James:
A Study in
Authentic Christianity

Eddie Rasnake

This book is dedicated to Terry Spinelli, my director as a new staff member with Cru at the University of Virginia. It was he who first encouraged me to start writing Bible studies.

Other books by Eddie Rasnake:
What Should I Do, Lord?
One Another: The Community God Wants Us To Be
Endangered Devotion
God is...

Working Thru The Word Series:
Righteousness of the Heart (The Sermon on the Mount – Matthew 5-7)
Radical Christianity (The Upper Room Discourse – John 13-17)
2 Corinthians
Colossians
James
Jude
Dangers to Devotion (Revelation 2-3)

Discipleship Series:
Becoming a Disciple
Becoming a Discipler
Becoming an Elder
The Devil, You Say?
God's Will
Transforming Truths
Where Do I Fit, Lord?

Following God Bible Study Series:
First Steps for the New Christian
Living God's Will
Ephesians
Romans
The Acts of the Holy Spirit 1 (1-12)
The Acts of the Holy Spirit 2 (13-28)
Using Your Spiritual Gifts
How to Develop a Quiet Time
Spiritual Warfare
Loving One Another

Following God: Co-Authored with Wayne Barber and Rick Shepherd
Women of the Bible – Book 1
Women of the Bible – Book 2
Life Principles from the Old Testament
Kings of the Old Testament
Prophets of the Old Testament
Men of the New Testament
Life Principles for Worship from the Tabernacle

Co-Authored with Michele Rasnake
Held in His Grace: A Young Mother's Journey Through Cancer

CONTENTS

Introduction

Background Assignment

Read the book of James through in one sitting at least three different times using several different translations of the Bible. What do you see as the "Big Idea" of this passage - your theme?

*Author's Note - Although there are many fine translations of the Bible, for studying purposes I would recommend the New American Standard Version or the Christian Standard Version. The method of translation (word for word) with these versions is perhaps not as easy to read as the New International Version (which is translated phrase for phrase), but is more technically exact for Bible study. It is recent enough as well to have made use of the more contemporary discoveries of manuscripts, which allows it to be more accurate than the King James version. Because the study questions are written to use with the NASB, you may need to reference it if you have difficulty because of using another version

LESSON ONE

"JAMES, BROTHER OF JESUS"

James 1:1

The book of James has been likened to the Old Testament book of Proverbs because of its emphasis on practical wisdom. It was probably the first of the New Testament epistles to be written (about AD 46) and is very Jewish in flavor. It also shares a great similarity to Jesus' "Sermon on the Mount" with at least ten direct parallels. Martin Luther thought little of the book at first, calling it "a right strawy epistle, having no true evangelical character." Being deeply affected by the message of Romans, he bristled at James' emphasis on works. Luther's view changed in time, and he came to see James as a practical complement to Romans.

The author of this epistle is identified as *"James, a bondservant of God and of the Lord Jesus Christ"* (James 1:1). There are four men named James who are mentioned in the New Testament. James, the son of Alphaeus (Luke 6:15) and James the father of Judas (Luke 6:16) are ruled out as potential authors of this book because of the authoritative nature of the letter and the fact that the author is so well known that he needs no other introduction than his first name. James, the son of Zebedee and brother of John (Luke 3:14) is unlikely because he was martyred in A.D. 44 (Acts 12:1, 2) at the very beginning of the scattering spoken of here in verse 1. The letter of James probably wasn't written until A.D. 48-49 at the earliest. James, the younger brother of Jesus is the most likely candidate and is commonly accepted as the author of this epistle since he was the recognized leader of the mother church in Jerusalem (Acts 12:17; Galatians 1:18-19). He was not a believer in Christ during His earthly ministry, and in fact was probably antagonistic (Mark 3:21-35; John 7:2-8).

Can you imagine what it was like to grow up as the little brother of Jesus? You follow Him through school and He probably made perfect scores. Whenever you get into an argument with Him, you're always wrong. He never does anything bad, never gets into trouble. He never swears when He bangs His thumb with a hammer in the family carpentry shop. Whenever you do something wrong your mom probably says, "Why can't you be more like Jesus?" To make matters worse, He becomes a well-known speaker and begins to imply that He is God incarnate. Imagine trying to explain your brother to your friends. Finally, your family is disgraced when He is executed like a common criminal. This is how James grew up.

The family business in the home where James grew up was carpentry. In the days before power tools, the wood had to be cut, sawn and hewn by hand through hours of backbreaking labor. Carpenters were known to be quite strong. While most of the homes in Palestine were made of brick and mortar, carpenters were the ones sought for hewn support beams and rafters. Woodworking was applied in the building of carts (the word "carpenter" is actually a contraction of "cartpenter"), as well as making wooden tools, basic furniture, and various repair jobs. As we will see this week, this man James eventually became a devout follower of Christ as well as the chief leader of the mother church in Jerusalem. He is even author of one of the books of the Bible. And what is the theme of this book? Authentic faith—the real thing. We are ready to begin looking at James, the brother of Jesus. We will see what his life teaches about walking with God..

Growing Up With Jesus

📖 What does Mark 3:21 reveal about James and the rest of the family's initial response to Jesus' public ministry?

The obvious truth revealed here is that all of Jesus' siblings, James included, think He is crazy. Mark 3:19–21 says He goes into a house (most likely His home in Capernaum), and while He is there, great crowds again gather. His family in Nazareth ("His own people"), hearing of all that is going on go out (from Nazareth to Capernaum) seeking *"to lay hold of Him, for they said, 'He is out of His mind'"* (NKJV). Verse 21 in the New American Standard Bible says, "He *has lost His senses.*" The Greek word translated "lost his senses" means to lose one's mental stability. Something not quite as obvious here is that Jesus' siblings really do care for Him. Rather than abandoning Him or ignoring Him, the family goes out to take custody (care) of Him.

📖 Matthew 12:46–50, Mark 3:31–35, and Luke 8:19–21 are most likely three different gospel accounts of the same incident. Comparing them, write any observations you have about Jesus' family's view of His ministry.

Again, we see Jesus' family holding a posture of unbelief. Jesus' response here is significant. Essentially what He reveals in this account is that His family must grow accustomed to relating to Him as His followers do. Christ's response does not come out of an uncaring position but is intended to force them to move beyond the understanding they had of Him as He grew up.

📖 In John 7:1–10 we get our last glimpse of James and the rest of the brothers' unbelief. Read the passage and write what stands out to you.

Two important facts are revealed here about James and the other brothers. We learn in verses 3–4 that the brothers see Jesus as one who *"seeks to be known publicly,"* and essentially what they are asking Him to do is to prove Himself to the world. We also read in verse 5 that *"not even His brothers were believing in Him."*

One important question—from what you know of Jesus' family, who is missing from all these verses that we have looked at today, and why do you suppose this is so?

Glaringly absent from each of these passages is any reference to Joseph, the father of the family. Most scholars believe that he had already died. This would mean that with Jesus going into public ministry, James has more responsibility in the household for a time as the oldest male at home, and perhaps he resents this.

It is easy for us to condemn Jesus' family for their initial unbelief, but it takes very little reflection to begin identifying with it. Regardless of what a person goes on to accomplish in their lifetime, the family always tends to view them in the role they have in that relationship. Add to this the difficulty anyone would have accepting the idea that God would become a human, and it is easier to understand the struggle that faces James and his siblings. During the remainder of this lesson on James, we will focus on the transformation that James experiences in his faith as he moves from seeing Jesus as His brother to recognizing Him as his Savior and Lord.

A Change in Thinking About Jesus

Although most of Jesus' family do not believe in Him during His earthly ministry, it is significant that all of them end up becoming believers. James and the rest of Jesus' family had undoubtedly heard the testimony of their parents about the uniqueness of Jesus' birth. They would have witnessed and/or heard about many of His miracles. But the most convincing evidence of all is His resurrection from the dead. From that point forward there is no mention of any more doubts about His divinity. Let's look at the process of how James and the others come to believe in Christ as the Son of God.
📖 Read John 19:26–27. Identify the context of these verses and write your thoughts on why James was not given the care of his mother.

This passage obviously reflects the special relationship that exists between Jesus and John, the disciple whom He loves. Mary's presence here and the connection with John suggest that she is now a believer. The fact that James is not given this responsibility implies that he is not yet a believer. Jesus undoubtedly has a reason for bypassing his brothers as caretakers of His mother.

📖 We next see James mentioned in Acts 1:14. Read this verse, along with the surrounding context, and write what you learn about James.

From this passage we can see that James is among those gathered in the Upper Room for prayer those ten days between Jesus' ascension and Pentecost. We are told that *these all with one mind were continually devoting themselves to prayer.* To be of "one mind" with the disciples, obviously means that James and the other brothers are all believers now. In 1 Corinthians 9:5, Paul links the brothers of the Lord with the apostles. James eventually earns the nickname "camel-knees" because his knees are so callused from kneeling in prayer.

📖 Now look at 1 Corinthians 15:7 and see what it suggests concerning what has brought about this change in belief for James.

Though not the first person to whom Jesus appears (Peter, then the whole group of disciples, and then some five hundred people all witness the risen Lord before James), he is specifically singled out for a post-resurrection appearance. Perhaps this is because James is so skeptical that only this will convince him. Maybe it is also because of the special role that James will play in the life of the early Church. In any case, the Lord comes to him and removes all doubt.

A Leader in Jerusalem

Nothing is said in Acts concerning how James assumed the role he holds in Jerusalem, but somewhere in the intervening years he rises to a position of prominence in the early Church. While the Lord's disciples focus on expansion of the faith, taking the gospel first to the Jews, then to the Samaritans, and ultimately to the Gentiles, James stays in Jerusalem. He has moved from mere sibling to skeptic to prayer participant to the recognized leader of the church in Jerusalem. With 3,000 souls converted on the day of Pentecost (Acts 2:41) and some 5,000 men coming to faith in one day a short time later, most theologians estimate that the church in Jerusalem has expanded very quickly to 20,000 or more people. James is at the helm of one of the largest congregations in history. This transformation of James from skeptic to leader has not happened overnight, but he certainly is a changed person by the time the Church is started. Today we want to study his leadership position and how James fills it as we look at the passages where he is mentioned.

📖 Look at Acts 12:17. Identify the context and write what you see here about James.

The context of this verse is the miraculous deliverance of Peter from prison. Once he fellowships with believers upon his return, his instruction is for them to *"Report these things to James and the brethren."* It is significant that he doesn't just say to report it to the brethren or to the leaders. Apparently, James is already the recognized leader of the church in Jerusalem. Equally significant is the fact that although Peter was the recognized leader of the disciples, he is not the main leader of the Jerusalem church.

📖 Read Galatians 1:18–19 and make note of what you learn about James.

We see here in Galatians that James spends some time with Paul three years after Paul's conversion. Probably they had already met, but the relationship is strengthened here. Paul identifies James in two significant ways: 1) as "the Lord's brother," and 2) as an apostle in Jerusalem.

Take a few minutes to read Acts 15:1–31. The new church is at a critical juncture. What was at first a body made up solely of Jews has begun to attract scores of Gentiles. The central question of the Jerusalem Council is "how does a Gentile come into the church?" Must he first become a Jew? Certainly, there is nothing wrong with the Jews continuing to honor the Law, provided that they recognize that the Law cannot save. For the Jewish Christians, neglect for the Law could offend the fellow Jews they are seeking to reach. But is it right to put the burden of the Law on the Gentiles, a burden which Peter says, "*neither our fathers nor we have been able to bear*"? Take a few minutes to answer the questions below and learn what you can about this circumstance of the Jerusalem Council.

📖 Looking at Acts 15:2, 4, and 6, exactly to whom do Paul and Barnabas address this question, and what do we know about them?

Three times the passage identifies the audience as the "*apostles and elders*" in Jerusalem. Jerusalem is the hub of the Jewish faith since the time of King David. With the birth of the church in Jerusalem, the city becomes the "home office," so to speak, of the Christian faith as well. The apostles spoken of here are those eyewitnesses of the resurrection who are the core leadership of the universal Church. The elders are separate and distinct from this group, though some apostles may also be elders. They are the leaders of the local church.

📖 Now look at Galatians 2:1–10 and identify who is reporting to whom. What else do you learn about the identity of these leaders.

It is noteworthy that Paul and Barnabas report to the church in Jerusalem to see if they have *"run in vain."* In other words, they trust the leadership there to make sure they are on the right track. From the leadership at Jerusalem, Paul identifies James, Cephas (Peter), and John as the key leaders and calls them "pillars." Most likely, these three men are listed in order of authority, placing James over Peter.

The Jerusalem Council

In Galatians 2:1–10, Paul details the visit to Jerusalem that he and Barnabas made before a group of men commonly called "The Jerusalem Council." At question was whether Gentile Christians needed to follow the Old Testament rite of circumcision. The conclusion of the council was a definitive answer of "no." One added suggestion, probably from James, was given though— *"to remember the poor"* (Galatians 2:10). The poor were always important to James. In his epistle he mentions them repeatedly with concern (1:9, 27; 2:2, 5–6, 15), while warning and admonishing the wealthy (1:10; 2:6,15–16; 4:1–4,13–16; 5:1–6).

📖 Look again at Acts 15.

Who had the final say in the debate (v. 13)?

What was his message (vv. 14–21)?

What resulted from the message (vv. 25, 31, 33)?
Many spoke on both sides of the issue, but it was James who seemed to be the moderator and the one who brought the discussion to closure. Notice that he took into consideration all the information that had been shared, but his answer hinged on what God had

already said. The result, according to the letter sent to Antioch, was that they had *"become of one mind"* (15:25). It is significant that Acts 15:28 credits the Holy Spirit with the Council's conclusion, indicating that the group recognized that God had spoken through James. The outcome was renewed rejoicing from the letter's encouragement (15:31), peace (15:33), and an unhindered continuation of the ministry of the Word of the Lord.

📖 What does Acts 21:18 reveal about the role of James in Jerusalem?

Although there was a plurality of elders in Jerusalem, James is clearly the principal leader at this time (probably AD 55–56). There is no mention of John or Peter as both men had probably left Jerusalem for reasons of safety and/or ministry.

📖 Read Galatians 2:11–12 and make note of what you learn of James from this passage. Be careful not to jump to conclusions. Simply observe the text.

We see here that certain men "from James" (who were obviously Jews) encouraged Peter to separate from the Gentiles. Although the men gave Peter bad advice, one important thing to learn about the incident is that the men were from James, implying that he was the leader of the church in Jerusalem.

📖 How does James identify himself in James 1:1?

What things are true about his relationship to Christ that he chose not to mention?

In beginning his epistle, James identifies himself as a "bond-servant" of God and of the Lord Jesus Christ. Remember that James is the brother of Christ, and yet he does not see himself in those terms. He sees his relationship to Christ not as a younger brother but as a devoted follower. Even though he is senior pastor of the mega-church in Jerusalem, he sees his service as unto God and unto Christ. A man of God may minister his call by serving people, but ultimately, he is called to serve God. Therefore, it is not the people, but God who defines one's service.

📖 Now, look at James 2:1, and make note of how he referred to his older brother.

James never refers to Jesus as the one with whom he grew up. Here he calls Him *"our glorious Lord Jesus Christ."* What a title of reverence! Paul writes in 2 Corinthians 5:16, *"Therefore from now on we recognize no man according to the flesh; even though we have known Christ according to the flesh, yet now we know Him thus no longer."* In like manner, James sees Jesus not through the eyes of the flesh, but through the eyes of the Spirit and of faith.

📖 James calls himself a "bond-servant." To us this may not mean much, but to a Jew reading this, it calls to mind a very specific type of relationship. Look up these Old Testament passages and write everything you can find out about "bond-slaves" or "bond-servants."

Exodus 21:5–6:

Deuteronomy 15:12–18:

The Hebrew Law permitted Jews to sell themselves into slavery for seven years as a means of paying off debt. If, at the end of that time, they felt that it would be beneficial to continue working for their master, they could choose to become a servant for life. Such an arrangement would be a two-way commitment. The servant would forever commit to do only the will of the master. The master would commit to provide for and to protect the bond-servant for as long as they live. The master would formalize this covenant relationship by piercing the ear of the "bond-servant" with an awl—providing visible evidence for any to see of the master-servant relationship.

📖 So, when James calls himself a "bond-servant of God and of the Lord Jesus Christ," what does he imply about himself (James 1:1)?

James essentially says that he has become a "slave" of God and of the Lord Jesus Christ. Notice that he identified Jesus as both his Lord and the Messiah. By identifying himself in this manner, James is saying that God has been such a good Master to him that he is thrilled to spend the rest of his life serving his Master, Jesus. Serving Jesus is not a requirement for James' salvation, but a loving response of gratitude for all that God has done in saving him. That is the way he lived his life until then end.

According to Josephus, and Hegesippus (a second century church historian): Shortly before Jerusalem was destroyed by the Roman army in 70 AD, during a time that many were coming to faith in

Christ, Ananus, the High Priest, assembled the Sanhedrin and commanded James, "the brother of Jesus who was called Christ," to proclaim from one of the galleries of the Temple that Jesus was not the Messiah. But instead, James cried out that Jesus was the Son of God and Judge of the world. His enraged enemies hurled him to the ground and stoned him, till a worker ended his sufferings with a club, while he was on his knees praying, "Father, forgive them, they know not what they do."

Personal Application

Jesus is a tough act for James and His other brothers to follow. Indeed, each of us would struggle with our own identity as the younger sibling of Jesus. But clearly James is his own man. He comes to realize that Jesus is not just his brother; He is the Messiah. Thoroughly Jewish, James is well schooled in the Law, but he realizes that simply keeping the Law is not what a genuine faith is all about. Real faith—not just being religious—is about trusting Christ and cultivating a growing relationship with God through Him. In the book that bears his name, James lays out his formula for godliness by warning us not to be carried away and enticed by our own fleshly desires, but to let the trials of our lives drive us to God, seeking His wisdom. Having found God's wisdom, we must act on it and apply it to our own lives. We must prove ourselves "doers" of God's Word and not just "hearers" (James 1:22) who deceive themselves into thinking they are spiritual because of how much they know instead of concentrating on how they live. *"The root of the righteous yields fruit,"* we are told in Proverbs 12:12. James rather bluntly tells us that a genuine faith will reveal itself by good works. *"Show me your faith without the works, and I will show you my faith by my works"* (James 2:18). As a bondservant of Christ, his life is more than words. It is a day-by-day manifestation of a real faith that is seen in his good works.

Since the "root" of the righteous yields "fruit," we can draw some conclusions about the health of our root by the fruit it is bearing in our lives. In Galatians we are given two lists of "fruit" that can be helpful in evaluating the health of our spiritual roots. The first list is called "the deeds of the flesh" (Galatians 5:19–21). The second list is called "the fruit of the Spirit" (Galatians 5:22–23).

Take a look at each of these lists and place a number from 1–5 (1=seldom and 5=always) beside each item that shows up on a regular basis in your life.

The Deeds of the Flesh (Bad Fruits)
___ immorality	___ impurity	___ sensuality
___ idolatry	___ sorcery	___ enmities
___ strife	___ jealousy	___ outbursts of anger
___ disputes	___ dissensions	___ factions
___ envying	___ drunkenness	___ carousing

The Fruit of the Spirit (Good Fruits)
___ love	___ patience	___ faithfulness
___ joy	___ kindness	___ gentleness
___ peace	___ goodness	___ self-control

As you look at the fruit that normally shows up in your life, what does that tell you about where your roots are?

We won't change our shortcomings by gritting our teeth and trying harder. These fruits are merely the evidences that show where our roots are growing. Tying apples on a pine tree won't fool anyone about what kind of tree it is. In the same way, trying to "act" loving with an unloving heart won't change who we are. We can't fake patience or gentleness. Joy will not come because we try hard to be joyful. Real faith, the kind James lived and writes about, only comes from yielding our lives to Christ's control. James expresses his relationship with Christ this way: *"James, a bond-servant of God and of the Lord Jesus Christ."* In other words, he so loves the Lord that he is a servant by choice. A bondservant is one who chooses to surrender their freedom so that they can forever serve their kind and loving master. If we want our lives to reflect the fruit of the Spirit instead of the deeds of the flesh, we must walk in surrender like James.
Have you ever come to a place where you surrendered control of every area of your life to Christ?

If not, why not?

If so, are there areas you have taken back from His control that need to be surrendered afresh?

James earned the respect of all in Jerusalem for his godly manner of living, and his epistle focuses on what it means to be a righteous person, a person with an authentic faith. When James says, "*the effective prayer of a righteous man can accomplish much*" (James 5:16), he puts the focus not on having effective prayer but on being a righteous person. His point seems to be, "if you become righteous, your prayers will be effective." Often, we try to become godly by praying more, rather than realizing that doing things in this fashion is like "putting the cart before the horse." Our prayer life will never go any further than our walk with God. The more godly we become the more effective our prayers will be. What does your prayer life say about the progress of your spiritual maturity?

If your prayer life isn't what it ought to be, you won't change it by determining to pray harder. You will only change it as you grow in a real faith relationship with Christ, and that begins with surrender— becoming a "bondservant" like James. Why not spend some time right now in prayer? Lord, I thank You for the testimony of James and the reality of his faith. I want that kind of relationship with You. I want my roots to be so deeply grounded in You, that Your fruit is born in my life. You have been such a good and faithful Master to me, I want to be Your bondservant. For the rest of my life, I want to do always and only Your will, knowing that You will care for me and meet my needs. Give me a real faith. Amen.

LESSON TWO

"HAPPY TRIALS TO YOU!"

James 1:2-12

James writes this letter to *"the twelve tribes,"* meaning the twelve tribes of Israel, a different way of referring to the Jews. In Chapter 2, verse 1, James speaks of their faith in Jesus Christ, indicating that they were Jewish Christians. At this early date (about 49 A.D.) most all Christians were from Jewish backgrounds. We are told specifically that these Jewish believers were *"dispersed abroad"* (literally, "the dispersion"). This term appears with a definite article in the Greek New Testament, indicating that he speaks not of some general scattering (e.g. Joe got transferred and moved to Cana, Bill and Sue inherited some land in Bethlehem and moved away, Mary moved to the coast for her health, etc.), but of a specific, well-known scattering. The obvious implication is that he is referring to the scattering of Jewish Christians from Jerusalem because of the persecution associated with Saul of Tarsus that began with the martyrdom of Stephen. Here's the main point: They were in tough times and were separated from the mother church and their Christian friends. They needed the kind of encouragement and practical exhortation found in this epistle.

God's Purpose for Trials (James 1:2-4)

📖 Why should we "Consider it all joy" when we encounter trials?

James gives three important reasons for us to conclude it is a joy when we encounter trials. First, we are commanded to. This is not a suggestion, but an imperative. Second, he tells us that testing our faith produces endurance. Finally, he goes on to say that the result of endurance is that we become mature, complete, full-grown.

The word *"encounter"* has the idea of "stumble into." You can't schedule or plan for a trial. They always catch you unaware. They are the spiritual equivalent of a "pop quiz" in a classroom. The term *"various"* is also sometimes translated "manifold, multifaceted, or multicolored." It is the same word used in the Septuagint (Greek translation of the Old Testament) for Joseph's multicolored coat (Genesis 37:3). The point is this: Trials come in all shapes and sizes.

This same Greek word (*poikilos*) is used similarly by Peter of trials (1 Peter 1:6). Later in the same epistle Peter uses this word to describe God's grace (1 Peter 4:10), and in Ephesians Paul uses a strengthened form of this word to identify God's wisdom. It is an encouraging thought to realize that whatever the shape, size and color of our trial, God has the grace and wisdom to match.

So what exactly constitutes a trial? The Greek word for trials here (*peirasmois*) has the same root as the word translated "temptation" in 1:13. James' point seems to be that a trial can become a temptation based on how we respond. My definition of a trial is any situation or circumstance that I need to trust God in, and in which there is a possibility of not doing that. (even blessing can be a trial in that it can make it hard for my trust to be in God).

📖 What do you think it mean to here to "consider?"

The Greek word James uses here, *hegeomai*, is a mathematical term (hence it is translated "count" in the KJV) and means literally "to bring before the mind." In other words, the call is to think about all the components of our situation, to add them all up, and to conclude that our trial is joy. It doesn't mean to "reckon" or believe in faith (although this aspect may be included by virtue of it being a command) but more to wrestle with it until you can conclude it is joy. It is not a natural reaction to consider it joy when we face hard times. It is normal to count it joy when we escape trials, not encounter them. It is worth reminding ourselves, however, that "joy" is a fruit of the Spirit (Galatians 5:22-23) and is therefore not bound to our circumstances, but to our relationship with God.

In the Septuagint (The Greek translation of the Old Testament) this same Greek word James uses to describe our trials (*poikilos* – translated "various" in 1:2) is used for Joseph's multi-colored coat. It means manifold, multi-colored, or multi-faceted. It can mean many different kinds of trials or trials with many dimensions, or both.

📖 What assumptions does James make in verse 2 about our experiences?

James states that we are to consider it all joy *"when"* we encounter various trials (not if). The assumption is that we will be encountering trials; they are inevitable and universal.

📖 What should we know as we approach trials?

Why should we know this?

Verse 3 says "knowing that the testing (the same root word in Greek as "approved" in verse 12) of your faith produces endurance." In other words, faith is like a muscle and exercising it produces endurance. Life experience should have taught us to value the lessons learned in adversity. Right thinking (doctrine) is what produces right acting. Knowing the results of acting rightly gives us something to hold on to, and helps us to maintain perspective so we can cooperate with God's process for maturity.

📖 How will that knowledge of the results of our testing help?

Knowing that our testing will strengthen our endurance helps us to keep our eyes on God instead of focusing solely on the trial. It gives us some of the "why" behind God allowing the difficulty into our lives, and thus makes it easier to "consider it all joy." Let me attempt to further explain this with an analogy: A man's best friend stabs him in the stomach with a knife. It sounds like a tragedy at this point with only limited information. Add to this the knowledge that the man's best friend was a doctor and was removing his ruptured appendix and the entire circumstance is reframed. The pain is no less real, but our perspective is completely changed. My point is this: God is our friend. Trials are His scalpel, and the only reason He undertakes such a painful process is for our good (see Jeremiah 29:11). He knows the pain is necessary to accomplish the benefit of the surgery.

📖 What is the "perfect result" of endurance?

The perfect result (singular – meaning the result of each individual trial), is that we may be "perfect" and "complete," and lacking in nothing with regard to the faith. "Perfect" here in 1:4 (Greek – *teleios*) means "adult, full-grown, achieving our full potential." It can be used in an absolute sense (i.e. God's perfection) or a relative sense as it is here. By relative I do not mean relative to each other so much as relative to our individual potential; to being where we ought to be. This idea is seen in the word, "complete" in verse 4 (Greek – *holokleros*, from *holos* meaning whole, and *kleros* meaning "with all that has fallen by lot, that which retains all which was allotted to it).

📖 What is God's process for us to respond to trials (Identify the progression of steps in verses 2-4)?

First, we are to know that testing produces endurance (it is implied that this has already happened before we "consider" them thusly). The second step in the progression is that we "encounter trials." Next, we are to reflect long enough on them spiritually to be able to "consider them joy." The next part of the progression is to "let endurance have its perfect result" – in other words, cooperate with what God is trying to do. In every trial there are two possible responses: enduring (trusting God) or escaping (trusting self or others instead of God). Enduring means more than simply tolerating the trial. It means actively putting our trust in God in the midst of the trial. So how do we do all of this? In order to accomplish each of the steps of this progression, we must act on the call to "ask God for wisdom." Trials create a need for God's perspective

In light of the truth in these verses, take some time to reflect on what you should being doing differently in your current circumstances.

God's Provision for Trials (1:5-8)

📖 What kind of need do our trials create in our lives?

Why?

A little Greek lesson may be helpful at this point to fully understand the "if" at the beginning of verse 5. There are three basic types of conditional statements in the Greek language that can be translated "if." The first class conditional "if" means "if, and it is true" or "since". The second class conditional is used when the supposition is contrary to fact ("if, and it is not true"). The third class conditional is utilized to communicate something which is probable but uncertain because it is future ("if, and it may be true). The "if" used here in James 1:5 is "first class conditional," meaning "since you lack wisdom." We do not have the wisdom to handle our trials unless God gives it to us. Wisdom is not merely information or knowledge, but knowledge applied to life.

The bottom line is this: I have no control over what life throws at me, but I do have control over how I respond to what life throws at me. To respond rightly, I have a need for wisdom: "what do I do?" I need God's wisdom so that I will cooperate with what God is doing and will "let" the trial have it's perfect result. Conversely, if we do not cooperate, it is logical to assume God will engineer another trial to accomplish the same result.

📖 How do we appropriate God's provision for this need?

Appropriating the needed wisdom only requires that we ask God (see Proverbs 3:5). We are to ask in faith, expecting His answer instead of doubting. The wrong response is not that we do nothing, but rather, that we try to solve the trial with our own wisdom (self-sufficiency) instead of drawing on God's.

📖 What does this passage tell us about God's character?

First, James tells us that God gives – present tense (continuously). He tells us God gives to all men, indicating that the provision of wisdom is based on grace rather than merit. James tells us that God grants wisdom generously (a better translation would be "freely" or "unconditionally") and without reproach or rebuke. James conveys the idea that God is on our side and wants us to succeed not fail. We don't have to fear that He will think us stupid for asking or talk down to us when we come to Him for help.

📖 What are the results of asking with a lack of faith?

James' wording here of the doubting one gives the ideas of a ship in a storm, unstable and battered by circumstances, out of control. It also says that he will be unstable in all his ways, not just in the trial. The passage says not to expect to receive anything. Usually in New Testament Greek, when an imperative is combined with a negative statement as it is here, what is being communicated is more than just a charge to not do something. Generally with this construction, the admonition is calling the reader to stop doing something

📖 What do you think it means here to be double-minded?

The particular Greek term James employs here (*dipsuchos*) literally means to be "two-souled." The word meaning conveys the idea of having divided allegiance and in 4:8 James ties in the idea of being half for the world and half for God (for further study see also Psalm 86:11 and Luke 11:17). To be double-minded is to be divided, wavering, at variance with oneself. Practically speaking, James' point seems to warn against being half-way committed to trusting God. Don't say you are trusting God if you are also working on plan B in case He doesn't come through like you want Him to.

In light of the truth in these verses, what sould you be doing differently?

God's Perspective on Trials (1:9-11)

📖 What point is James making to the "brother of humble circumstances"?

By employing the term, brother, James indicates he is speaking of a believer. Although most translations use a phrase such as "humble circumstances" to speak of this man, a literal rendering would simply be the "humble" brother, but the contrast with the rich man implies that James has a man of humble means financially in view. Poor is a purely temporal definition, for it has in view only worldly goods. Likewise, to call one "rich" is only in reference to material goods. It has no bearing on the person's worth before God. James instructs the poor man to glory in or value that in his life which is eternal (his position with God) and look beyond his immediate circumstances.

📖 What do you think the "high position" is in which the poor believer is to glory?

Do you see any application to those who aren't poor?

The humble believer is to "glory" in his or her high position, which would seem to be their position in Christ – their eternal standing (see Ephesians 1:3-14; 1 Peter 2:9-10). He or she is chosen by God, adopted into His family, loved, redeemed and forgiven, sealed, given an inheritance, etc. (see also Revelation 2:9 and 2 Corinthians 6:10). To "glory" has the idea of boasting or bragging, and grammatically, this call is in the imperative mood – he or she is commanded to boast. Why? Because God has worked in their life. All of us need to recognize these things and view them as real wealth.

📖 What point is James making to the rich man?

The person of means needs to recognize that in his or her life which is temporal (wealth and security) and look beyond those things. They need to not place their trust in temporal wealth. Nothing truly belongs to a person which can be taken away.

📖 What do you think it means for the rich person to "glory in his humiliation"?

The person of temporal wealth is to rejoice (glory) in that which humbles – either loss of wealth or trials which show the transitory nature of wealth. The rich man is to boast or brag about the fact that their riches (the reasons the world calls them rich) are temporary like a flower that blooms and then withers. Nature teaches an endless lesson reminding us that temporal things won't last and are not eternal.

The treatment of wealth and poverty here in the context of trials suggests an interesting application. It would appear James is suggesting that blessing can be as much of a trial as adversity. Remember the definition we presented earlier of a trial: "Any situation or circumstance that I need to trust God in, and in which there is the possibility of not doing that." Blessing fits that description as well as adversity. For example, winning the lottery could be a real trial as it could easily distract us away from putting our trust in God.

📖 Do you see any applications to those who aren't rich?

Each of us, regardless of our material circumstances, needs to recognize these principles and identify how their perspective might be skewed by the distorted value system of our society. I find it interesting that the material humans place so much value in on earth (gold) is used for asphalt in heaven.

📖 Looking again at verses 9-11, what in this passage is permanent?

What in this passage is perishable?

The issue with the contrast here is not that poverty is always spiritual and that wealth is always sinful, but that either circumstance must be viewed in light of eternity. The emphasis is on each person's spiritual circumstances, not on the dollars and cents involved. All the things of this world will pass away. Anything that is not eternal is eternally insignificant.

Conclusion (1:12)

📖 What is the blessing given here in James 1:12?

The language of this verse is in the form of a beatitude. To be "blessed" differs from happiness in that it is not merely the result of favorable circumstances. A blessed (*makarios*) person is one whom God makes fully satisfied, not because of favorable circumstances, but because He indwells the believer through Christ. To be blessed, is equivalent to having God's kingdom within one's heart. The grammar indicates the passing of a verdict, and promises the "crown of life" to those who are approved.

📖 How, according to James, are we approved?

Several ideas emerge as we reflect on this statement. First, it clearly indicates that the trial will not last forever. There will come a point when it is over. The longest we will have to endure any trial is until the day of Christ. Many less than that. Second, the implication is that it truly matters whether or not we trust God through the testing.

James clearly states that the blessing he speaks of is the reward to the one who perseveres." The action verb here is in the present tense (meaning continuous or repeated action, not a one-shot act), and the active voice (the approved one is not just passively letting things happen to them, but actively trusts God as they deal with the trial). To persevere means "to remain under, to go the distance and not bail out under the trial."

📖 What is the "crown of life" James speaks of as the reward here?

The word "crown" here (*stephanos*) does not mean a crown like a king would wear (*diadem*), but rather, is the word for a wreath or garland awarded the winner of a race or a prize. It has the idea of something earned, not merely something bestowed. James' point is that it will be worth it to trust God and obey Him, for we will be rewarded. The Greek phrasing is literally the "crown consisting of life" and may refer to future reward but also ties in the idea of present experience. Once we have successfully endured the trial there is a freshness and joy to life on the other side that wasn't possible before. As we have already seen, one of the purposes of trials is to make us more like Jesus. The more we cooperate with God in our trials, the more He makes us like Jesus. The more we become like Jesus, the more we experience victory. As God works in our lives through our trials, our character is changed. Once that has happened, we have relief even if our circumstances are not changed. This relief of changed character is strongly suggested by the word "blessed". There is also clear evidence of a specific future reward called "the crown of life" since the definite article is used (see Revelation 2:10). In heaven, believers will receive crowns which may then be used to worship Christ by laying them at His feet. Those without such crowns will come to Him empty-handed.

Personal Application

One of the greatest test of Authentic Christianity is how it responds to the day-to-day challenges of life. Ron Dunn once said; "you can have victory over self, and you can have victory over sin, and you can have victory over Satan, but unless you have victory over situations you're still missing out." The Christian life isn't lived on a mountain top but in the everyday humdrum of paying bills and finding a parking space – of fighting the flu and final exams. The real issue is "Does your Christian Faith make a difference there?" If it does then the world will stop and notice - if not, then you need help. James tells us that authentic Christianity draws on God's wisdom to face every situation of life. These questions are meant to aid in that process.

1. What trails are you experiencing now? (be specific)

2. How can you apply James 1:1-12 to one or more of these trials? (again, try to be specific)

A. By your attitude

B. By your asking

LESSON THREE

"A LIFE AND DEATH DECISION"

James 1:12-21

During the late 1970's the FBI performed an investigation of U.S. Congressmen called "ABSCAM". Undercover agents posed as foreign diplomats and infiltrated the confidence of Congressmen. Once on the inside, they then offered the congressmen bribes in exchange for certain favors in terms of their voting. So the bait was set before them. Would they bite, or would they back off? Unfortunately, many sunk their teeth right into the bait, and as a result, were hooked and hauled in.

Whether you consider these men unfair victims of a terrible trap set by the FBI, or just terribly guilty for what they did, one thing is clear. Each man had a test placed before him - an opportunity. An opportunity either to reveal their true character as one worthy of their elected office, or... to fail the test. A choice had to be made when that test was placed before them - that opportunity was part of the test. Now, the integrity that was put on the line was either going to be shown intact, or it would be shown to be a failure. In facing that bait, they had a decision - either they were going to respond to the test in a way that demonstrated their value, or they would fail. They would demonstrate that their convictions could be captured by currency.

The tragedy is that most of those men failed to realize the significance of their decision. They failed to realize that what they did would have such monumental consequences and results. If they refused the bribes, there would be the reward of approval and continued success in the political arena. They would be given the kind of publicity money can't buy. But if they yielded, there would be the ruin and destruction of a respectable career.

Most of us never experience someone coming into our office or home and offering such an opportunity, but we do experience the test of relationships with co-workers. We do experience the test of bosses with unrealistic expectations. We've all experienced the feeling when there is a lot of month left at the end of our money. Much in the same way as those congressmen, we have the opportunity to respond to tests, but often we fail, just like the congressmen, to realize the results of the way we react to our tests.

The Right Reaction (1:12)

 According to this verse what is the right reaction to trials?

James tells us that the correct reaction when trials enter our experience is to persevere under the trial until it is through, learning what God desires us to.. The Greek word (*hupomeno*, from *hupo*, under, and *meno*, to remain) carries the meaning to remain under, to go the distance and not bail out. It is in the present tense (continuous action) and the active voice – meaning not passive toleration but active trust in God.

 Will this person get relief from their trials and if so, how?

God's purpose for allowing a trial into our lives is to change our character. When this purpose has been realized, it gives relief because the changed character enables us to be victorious in the trial.

Eventually, whether on earth or in heaven, there is relief as well when the trial ends.

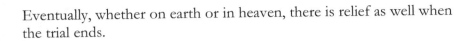 How will this person who perseveres be rewarded?

The one who perseveres in their trial will receive the promised "crown of life" once he or she has been approved (shown genuine). As we discussed in the last lesson, this may mean future reward in the form of crowns in heaven, or the present reward of the abundant life, or both. In speaking of this crown of life, James clarifies, "...which the Lord has promised to those who love Him." Our response to trials can be an act of worship and is a way to express our love for God (see John 14:15).

The Wrong Reaction (1:13-18)

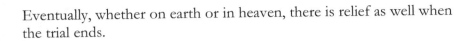 According to this passage, what is right thinking toward God in the midst of a trial or temptation?

God cannot be persuaded to do evil – He is untemptable (Greek: *apeiraztos* – *a*, without, and *peirazo*, to tempt or test). Because of this, He cannot be involved in persuading us or anyone else to do evil. Understanding this reframes our view of the trials He allows. Since God can never have an evil motive, His goal in our trials is always our success, not our failure. Since He is all-knowing and all-powerful, He can filter out any trials where we do not have a chance to succeed. The phrase, "He Himself does not tempt anyone" appears in the emphatic position in the text. God tempts (solicits to evil) absolutely no one.

📖 Is it possible for God to be involved in tempting?

It is not possible for God to be involved in tempting anyone to sin or evil. It would contradict His character. Because of this, we can logically conclude that the only reason He gives us trials is for us to succeed (endure) not to fail (be enticed). The Greek word translated "tempted" here (*peirazo*) shares the same root as the word translated "trial" in verse 2 (*peirazmos*), though the meanings are very different. They are differentiated only by their usage. This would suggest that it is possible for a trial (that which God allows) to become a temptation (a solicitation to evil) depending on how we respond.

📖 Verse 14 uses fishing or hunting terms (enticed, carried away) to describe temptation. What similarities do you see between these and temptation?

"Carried away", (a Greek hunting or fishing term meaning to be drawn away, lured to bait), is in the present tense (continuous action) and the passive voice (to be acted on by an outside agent). Our flesh is the agent here ("by his own lusts") and can draw us away from the Spirit's leading. "Enticed", (also a Greek hunting or fishing term) suggests to draw and entice or catch with bait. It is used in the present tense (continuous) and the middle voice (I participate in the results of the action). Our flesh can entice us toward sin. In fishing, bait has two purposes a) to heighten interest and b) to hide the hook. The lure is deceiving because it promises one thing (a free meal) but delivers something else (entrapment). Like the fish, if we give in the result is death.

📖 Who is to blame for sin according to these verses?

The real blame for sin lies not in the temptation but in a person's lust. Without the lust the temptation wouldn't mean anything. Therefore, the one who falls can't say "the devil made me do it". Notice that James lays the blame for sin squarely on the shoulders of the believer ("by his own lusts"). He makes it clear God is not to blame, and if James believed a demon were to blame, he would have included that. When I sin, it is by my own choice, and I can blame no one else. This is the message of 1 Corinthians 10:13 where we read, "No temptation has overtaken you but such as is common to man; and God is faithful, who will not allow you to be tempted beyond what you are able, but with the temptation will provide the way of escape also, so that you will be able to endure it." His faithfulness is on the line with each trial He sends our way, and He determines we are able, by faith and perseverance, to succeed or He doesn't allow it in our lives.

📖 Verse 15 uses child-bearing language to describe the sin process. What are some logical illustrations that can be drawn from this analogy?

There are some interesting parallels between the process of conceiving and giving birth to a child, and the process of giving in to sin. It takes a union between the circumstance (temptation) and our fallen desires (lust) to produce sin. This union is the conception and happens internally (in the mind). The delivery (actions) is the external part of this equation, and if this child (sin) is not aborted, the result is death (spiritual death), a loss of fellowship with God (see also Romans 7:1-6).

📖 Explain in your own words the progression and consequences of yielding to temptation.

The process of sin begins with deception or temptation (being carried away and enticed). Conception (the joining of lust and temptation in the mind) occurs next. At this point, the sin only exists in the form of an improper attitude. Unless there is repentance, we then give birth to sin (the wrong actions begin). Over time, in the absence of true, heart-felt repentance, sin is fully accomplished. Death is brought into our walk – we break fellowship with God. It is important to realize that the Western mindset of death (something ceases to exist) is incorrect. In a Biblical sense, death does not mean cessation, but separation. The soul that dies in sin does not cease to exist. It will continue to exist for all eternity, but in a state of separation from God. As believers, we cannot lose our permanent relationship with God because of sin, but we can temporarily lose our fellowship with Him.

📖 Contrast the results of verse 12 (the right reaction) and verses 14 and 15 (the wrong reaction).

When we endure and trust God in the midst of a trial or temptation, the result is the crown of life. When we are enticed to sin, the result is death. Therefore, temptation really is a life and death decision.

📖 Compare verse 5 and verse 14. Who can we choose to listen to in our trial?

James 1:5 makes it clear that we can and should listen to the Lord in the midst of a trial, drawing on His wisdom through prayer. In verse 14 we see that instead, we can choose to listen to our own lusts and selfish desires. The life or death decision is whether we listen to the Lord or our lusts.

📖 How could we become deceived according to verse 16?

James' charge, "do not be deceived" alerts us that there is the potential I might be deceived. This statement is in the imperative mood (a command) and active voice (I am in control of the action). James' point is this: "Don't allow yourself to be deceived (to be led astray)." We could become deceived by accepting that which is not true, or by rejecting that which is true, or both. The Greek word here (*planao*) means "to cause to wander, to lead astray" (from *plane*, a wandering).

📖 What in verses 17 and 18 could we become deceived about?

Think of how intensely practical James' warning is here. In the midst of a trial, we could be tempted to believe that God and His gifts are not good. Another error of believe is the wrong idea that good could have any source other than God. A third incorrect belief is that it is possible for God to change. There is no "variation or shifting shadow" to Him (carrying the idea of a sundial). Unlike everything else, God never changes, so He always and only gives good gifts. There is no possibility of anything else. In a trial we could also wrongly conclude that God doesn't have a will for us, or that His Word is not truth, or that we aren't His creation.

God is working by His will and for His glory through our salvation. Why would He work against that by tempting us to evil?

The Response Required (1:19-20)

📖 Compare and contrast all references in the chapter to speaking and hearing. Who should we be quick to hear and why?

In light of the context, it would seem that the call to be "quick to hear" is to be quick (swift) to hear God (1:5) rather than our own lusts (1:14), because He is good (1:17), untemptable and doesn't tempt (1:13), unchanging (1:17), and His word is truth (1:18). Also, it is good to remind ourselves that it is impossible to do God's will until we have heard from Him.

📖 Why should we be slow to speak and about what?

We are to be "slow to speak" or slow to jump to conclusions because this inhibits hearing God. You can't speak and hear at the same time and when we speak quickly we tend to say the wrong things, especially about God and our trials (1:13). We need to wait to speak and draw conclusions about God and our trials until we have His perspective. Otherwise we will tend toward anger. We are called to be "slow to anger". Each of the three admonitions of verse 19 counter our natural or fleshly reactions: a) to not hear God, b) to speak against God either directly or by speaking against the trial He allowed, and c) to be angry against God and/or the trial.

The word used here for anger (*orge*) originally referred to any human emotion, and came to be associated with anger as the strongest of human emotions. One could legitimately substitute the word "emotions" or "feelings" here. In other words, his message is that following your feelings will not result in God's righteousness.

📖 What is God's overall purpose for us according to verse 20?

God's goal is for us as believers is that we would "achieve" His righteousness (become like Christ). To do this, we must stay in line with His objectives.

📖 How might we interfere with God's purpose for our lives according to this passage?

It is possible that we might interfere with God's purpose for our lives by deceiving ourselves by listening to ourselves and trying to solve our own problems instead of listening to God. By walking by our feelings (1:20) instead of walking by faith (1:6), we will separate from God's path and the wisdom He offers.

Conclusion (1:21)

📖 Identify the commands of this verse and consider how this call applies to you on a day-to-day basis.

James' call here is that we would put aside filthiness (specific acts), as well as all that remains of wickedness (our old sin nature), and receive God's word humbly and let it take root in our life. As we encounter trials, "in humility" we must admit our need. We must then "receive the Word", the wisdom God has for us. He will not force it on us. When the truth of God's Word, sown in the soil of our heart, is united by faith in us, it is "implanted" or engrafted into us. The result is that it is able to "save" our souls. This phrase speaks not of initial justification, but of the sanctification process, and may have in view our sanctification as it relates to the specific area of our trial.

Personal Application

In verses 1-12 James makes it clear that the right response to trials is to ask God for wisdom. In verses 13-20 he shows the wrong response – listening to our own lusts. With those two principles you see the foundational challenge of Christianity. Every day in every situation we make a decision to follow God or to follow our own selfish desires. If we persevere and follow God the result is "life" (verse 12). If we are enticed by our own lusts and give in to sin the result is "death" (verse 15). So it really is a life and death decision – one that we often take too lightly. Consider the following questions as you evaluate your own life and death decisions.

1. Have you contemplated the effects of your
   response to trials before?

2. Have you experienced the exhilaration of faithfully enduring a trial?

3. When you have failed to endure, what were some of the consequences?

Evaluation

1. Right now, are you enduring or being enticed in the midst of your trials?

Enduring 1 2 3 4 5 6 7 8 9 10   Enticed

2. What do you need to do to handle the temptations you are presently experiencing?

_____ Admit my own responsibility

_____ Consider the consequences of yielding

_____ Have right thinking about God

3. What specific actions, if any, do you need to take in light of this passage?

A. What do I need to put aside?

B. What of the Word do I need to receive?

LESSON FOUR

"OBEDIENCE – DO YOU DO?"

James 1:19-27

Charles Colson, the former White House counsel and Watergate co-conspiritor, came to Christ as a result of his trial and conviction. He later started a ministry to the incarcerated called Prison Fellowship. He became one of the preeminent Christian voices of his generation. He wrote a challenging article entitled "How the Pro-Life Protest has Backfired" which seems to speak directly to the idea of our anger not achieving God's righteous purposes. He wrote...

"I've opposed abortion ever since I knew what it was. When I committed my life to Christ...my moral convictions deepened...That is why I have fervently supported the efforts of the thousands of Christians who protest at abortion clinics. ...But I have grown increasingly uneasy about the conduct of some involved in this movement...Rather than piercing anyone's conscience, I wonder if we are not stabbing both our neighbor and the cause instead. ...I...well understand that editors can select the most offensive photos that caricature Christians. But even so, our stridency has played into their hands. ...News footage of Christians screaming and waving their Bibles, faces twisted with hate and anger, hardly helps our cause. ...We must woo people's hearts toward righteousness. But we cannot woo unless we love. It is more than the battle against abortion that suffers when Christians conduct themselves with anger and hate. We wound our witness of the truth of the gospel and the love of Jesus Christ."

"A friend recently told me the tragic story of a young woman who was brutally beaten and raped. Though she lived, she is now beset by nightmares, severe emotional trauma, and stress. And some weeks after her assault, she discovered that as a result of the rape, she was pregnant. This young woman is a Christian, opposed to abortion. Yet the violence of her attack was destroying her. She sought pastoral counseling, and then, sincerely believing she could not emotionally survive the pregnancy, made the anguished decision to abort. On the appointed morning, she miserably made her way to an abortion clinic. There she encountered a group of protesting Christians, who, as she walked slowly toward the clinic doors, pointed and shouted angrily at her across the barricade: 'Murderer! Murderer! Murderer!' Those shouts of hate did nothing to change the girl's decision. They did, however, rub salt into her raw wounds."

James 1:20 tells us that "the anger of man does not achieve the righteousness of God." If our actions are not a direct result of responding to having heard from God, but instead are responding to the promptings of our flesh, we may damage and destroy instead of minister. Let's take a closer look at what James has to say about doing what we think is right without really hearing from God.

Doing Without Hearing Equals Self-will (1:19-22)

📖 Who or what do you think we are called to hear in verse 19, and why did you draw that conclusion?

In light of the context, it would seem that the call is to be quick ("swift") to hear what God is saying (see 1:5). When we ask God for wisdom in our trial, verse 5 promises He will give it. If we don't hear God, our actions will be driven by our own passions and probably won't be right. The admonition in verse 21 to receive the Word indicates the primary way in which we hear God.

📖 What happens if we try to do what is right without hearing?

When we try to do what is right without hearing God first, we are following our own will and wisdom instead of His. Therefore, it becomes impossible for us to endure trials since we don't know how to do it God's way, and we become fair game to temptation of some kind. With the word "temptation" our minds run to overt iniquity, but the enticement isn't always just to gross sin. It may be to self-dependence or some other human attempt at coping.

📖 What does God want, our attention or our action, and how does He want it?

God desire both our attention and our action, but He needs our attention first so our actions follow His will instead of our own. We are to be "slow to speak", or slow to jump to conclusions because this inhibits hearing God. With the call to be "slow to anger", the implication is patience. Each of the three admonitions of verse 19 counter our natural or fleshly reactions: a) to not hear God, b) to speak against God either directly or by speaking against the trial He allowed, and c) to be angry against God and/or the trial.

📖 How does the "anger of man" keep us from achieving the "righteousness of God"?

What do these terms mean?

God works His will out in our lives when we are patient, not when we are angry. Anger is not usually a response. It is a reaction fueled by emotion, not volition, and it moves others to react instead of respond. Anger here is from the Greek word "*orge*" (the origin of our English word "orgy") and originally meant any human emotion or feeling, and came to be associated with anger which was considered by the Greeks to be the strongest of human passions. The "righteousness of God" refers ultimately to sanctification or Christ-likeness. God's goal is for us to "achieve" His righteousness (become like Christ – see Romans 8:28-30). For this goal to be realized, we must be in line with how He is working and what He is working toward.

How do we "put aside" filthiness and wickedness?

Why should we do this first?

James is into an agricultural analogy, that of a seed planted in fertile soil. He is probably drawing on Jesus' parable of the sower as he writes. In this analogy there are two parts which are reflected in the passage: We must Prepare the soil by "putting aside all filthiness." This seems to have in view specific sinful acts. To "put aside" means to "put off from oneself, to separate oneself from" and we do this by a lifestyle of confessing and repenting as God reveals areas to us. The phrase, "and all that remains of wickedness" points to all that is left of our old sin nature. When accompanied with "humbly receiving the implanted word," this offers an excellent picture of how to maintain fellowship with God and to grow spiritually.

📖 How is the word "implanted" and what fruit does this tree grow?

We must plant the seed of God's Word in "humility." Practically speaking, we must admit our need. The Word takes root in our lives if we have first dealt with unconfessed sin, when we receive it humbly (1:21) by a request (1:5) of faith (1:6). James says we must "receive the Word." God will not force it on us. He also conveys that the Word must be "implanted" or engrafted, sown in the soil of our heart. The purpose of trials is to give us opportunities to do this and to move us in this direction. The resulting fruit is righteousness (see 3:18) as we both hear and obey.

📖 What are some examples of deluding ourselves by hearing without doing?

We can be deluding ourselves when we say we were "blessed" by a sermon or message then doing nothing with it. Another way we can delude ourselves with truth is when we know the right thing to do (e.g. prayer, evangelism) but do not act or change our behavior.

The Greek word "prove" here (*ginomai*) has the idea of "become." It appears in the present tense (continuous action), the active voice (I must do it), and the imperative mood (a command, not a suggestion).

The Greek word translated "delude" here is *paralogizomai* (*para*, alongside, and *logizomai*, logic or reasoning) and means to miss the mark of logic, reason, or truth. Knowledge that is not acted on is not only of no benefit to me, but it also can be a detriment. It can become a deluding influence, deceiving me into thinking I am spiritual because of what I know instead of because of how I live. Because of this, verse 22 is key to the whole section and chapter. It is the primary application point around which every other one revolves.

Hearing Without Doing Equals Self-deception (1:23-25)

Psychologist David Myers, in his article, "The Inflated Self" (THE CHRISTIAN CENTURY, 1 December 1982, p.1226-8), reveals some startling evidence regarding man's perception of himself. Unlike the "New Age" assertion that a person's greatest problem as ignorance of his or her potential and divineness, Myers' evidence points out that humanity's real problem is an inflated view of self. His research reveals that almost all people see themselves as better than average. Most American business people see themselves as more ethical than most; most community residents view themselves as less prejudiced than others; and most drivers assume that they are better-than-average drivers. When asked to rate themselves, ZERO percent of the 829,000 students who answered the poll thought themselves below average, 60% saw themselves in the top 10%, and 25% rated themselves in the top 1% of their class.

Researcher Steven Sherman called residents of Bloomington, Indiana, asking what they would do if called to volunteer three hours to an American Cancer Society drive. One half responded that they would help if asked. When he called a comparable group of residents actually requesting they help, only four percent agreed.

Each of us needs to acknowledge how easily our flesh can deceive us. James makes it clear that if we know what is right, but don't do it, that knowledge becomes a deluding influence in our lives, deceiving us to think more highly of ourselves than is accurate. Hearing God and not doing equals self-deception.

📖 Describe the situation in verses 23 and 24 in your own words.

What does the person do right?

What do they do wrong?

The analogy James offers here seems to suggest a person who looks at their natural face (their physical features) in a mirror and sees that it is dirty but walks away and forgets it without taking any action. They look in the mirror to observe their appearance, which is right and appropriate, but they leave without taking any action and forget what they saw. What good does it do to see that you are dirty if you do nothing about it? The word James uses which is translated "looks" has the prefix *kata*, indicating this is not referring to a casual observer, but one who looks attentively.

James speaks of being a "hearer of the Word." Hearing the Law played a very important part in Jewish life. Jews thought of themselves as special and set apart because they possessed the Law of God, not always realizing that they were blessed by obeying it, not merely by hearing it. It is important to hear the Word so we aren't merely following ourselves, but it can't stop there. The person in James' illustration is a hearer of the Word but not a "doer." No earthly parent would be proud of a child who excelled at reciting his parents' directives but never obeyed them. In a real sense, hearing without doing is worse than not hearing at all, for with greater revelation comes greater accountability.

📖 What is the mirror allegorical of in James' illustration?

In James' analogy, the mirror represents the Word of God, which affords the Christian the opportunity to evaluate himself. This is a very descriptive symbol since it is in the Word that we are able to see ourselves from God's perspective and observe what needs to change.

📖 What does the "law of liberty" refer to here in James 1:25 and what does this title say about its nature?

The "law of liberty" mentioned here is the perfect (complete) law or the Word of God, and its nature (liberty) is reflected in the interwoven theme of grace. The translation literally reads "the law which gives liberty." The whole, mature law of God is liberating and freeing. If we don't see it as such, then we really haven't understood what Scripture is saying. James uses the beautiful adjective, "liberty," as an apt description of the nature of God's Word.

In your study of the Word are you one who "looks intently" or more a "forgetful hearer?"

📖 Do you think "looking intently" at the Word make one Blessed? Why or why not?

It is not reading the Bible alone that brings blessing, but "looking intently" and "abiding by it." Obedience to God brings the joy and blessing, and not merely the accumulation of spiritual information.

Hearing With Doing Equals Sanctification (1:25-27)

📖 Identify the progression of actions in verse 25.

The first step James identifies is to look intently at the perfect law (keeping its nature of grace in view). It is worth noting that the Greek word translated "looks intently" here is parakupto (para, beside, kupto, to bend) and has the idea of bending over, stooping down to examine something more closely. God's Word merits close scrutiny, not casual observance. Looking intently and the scriptures must be followed up with abiding by it as an effectual doer. The Greek term "abides" here (parameno, from para, beside, and meno, to remain or stay) means to stay beside or in line with God's Word. It is impossible to align ourselves with God's Word if we are not studying it. D.L. Moody put it this way: "The only way to keep a broken vessel full is to keep the faucet running." The two positive actions of looking intently and abiding are followed by a negative reminder: don't become a forgetful hearer, and a pronouncement that the result of all of these steps is blessing in what the person does.

A beatitude ("blessed") differs from happiness in that it is not merely the result of favorable circumstances. A blessed (makarios) person is one whom God makes fully satisfied, not because of favorable circumstances, but because He indwells the believer through Christ. To be blessed, is equivalent to having God's kingdom within one's heart. It is not the hearing of God's Word, nor the study of it, no matter how intense, which brings blessing. It is only as we abide by what God says (and most of what He has to say to us is found in Scripture) that we experience spiritual blessing.

📖 In light of this process, how is verse 26 a negative example?

The person in question thinks themselves to be religious yet their religion doesn't affect his or her actions. They have deceived their own heart to think they are spiritual when they aren't. The gist of James' illustration is that a person thinks of themselves as religious, but their religion has made no difference in what comes out of his or her mouth. By "religious", James means the outward practice of religion – in other words, the person thinks they are doing a good job in their faith.

📖 What is the result of this negative approach?

The result of this negative approach is a deceived heart and a worthless faith. The Greek word carries the meaning of "empty, hollow, useless, non-productive, that which does not accomplish it's intended purpose." Again, as in 1:22, we see James emphasize the fact that to hear God's Word and not obey it is to be in a state of self-deception. This verb "deceives" is in the present tense (continual) and active voice (something he does to himself). We see James introduce a contrast here that he will more fully develop in the next chapter: living faith (that which results in works) and dead faith (that which produces no results).

📖 Compare the example in verse 27 with the process in verse 25.

James identifies pure and undefiled religion (the Greek word *amiantos* has the idea of "unpolluted, free from contamination") with two specific behaviors. In contemporary Christian thought the term "religion" carries a somewhat negative connotation not implied in the word James selects. Here he is referring merely to the outward manifestations of inward faith. By looking to the Lord and His Word and then acting upon it as verse 25 exhorts, the believer is motivated to actions which God values even if the world does not.

James offers two evidences here of authentic faith. How is visiting orphans and widows a manifestation of pure and undefiled faith? First, we must understand that these were the most abused, underprivileged and neglected members of society in James' day. No one would pat you on the back for caring for their needs, nor would the widows or orphans be able to repay you in any way. The only motivation for such an act would be a desire to please God. The second evidence of genuine faith James mentions is keeping oneself unstained by the world. Like visiting orphans and widows, to keep oneself unstained (literally, "without spot") by the world (practical holiness) is not the kind of behavior people are going to congratulate you for. Choices of holiness are rarely noticed by anyone but God. The point of both of these evidences is not that they are the only way genuine faith manifests itself, but that they are two examples where you know they are not defiled by double motives. When He is the only audience our motives have to be pure or we won't bother to act.

Conclusion

📖 Identify the application points of verse 25 and consider how they apply to you on a day-to-day basis.

By way of review, the call is to look intently at the Word, and then abide by it, not forgetting what we see but taking action on it. Such a process is a good model for directing and measuring the quality of our time in God's Word.

📖 How does a life of obedience to the Word fit in the midst of trials and temptations?

The only way to adequately face the trials of life is by drawing on God's wisdom through Bible study and prayer and by taking action on what he leads us to do or tells us not to do.

With this first chapter James has related his major theme for the book which is his formula for authentic Christianity. Simply put, James' formula for walking with God is this: in every situation of life that we face we have two choices on how to deal with it. Either we can draw on God's wisdom resulting in an abundant life, or we can draw on our own wisdom resulting in spiritual death. If we choose to seek God's wisdom we must still choose to do what He says. This is the fundamental lesson of chapter one. The chapters that follow all build on this foundation. Rather than providing new theological treatises they give more examples of how the truths of chapter one are lived out in day-to-day life – a series of applications if you will. In light of this, it would be worthwhile to review the meat of chapter one briefly at this point.

Personal Application

As the prophet Samuel exhorted King Saul, "To obey is better than sacrifice, and to heed than the fat of rams. For rebellion (disobedience) is as the sin of divination (witchcraft), and insubordination (lack of submission) as iniquity and idolatry (putting something else before God)" – 1 Samuel 15:22-23. Lack of obedience to God's Word is a serious matter. The following questions are to motivate you to be obedient to God's Word.

1. Are you actively involved in hearing the Word?

2. What do you need to do to become a better hearer of the Word?

Use this graph to rate the quality of your hearing of the Word: (be honest)

Glance 1 2 3 4 5 6 7 8 9 10 Gaze
Casually Carefully

4. In what ways are you seeking to apply the Word of God?

5. Use this graph to rate your own obedience to the Word: (again, be honest)

Forgetful   Effectual

Hearer   1   2   3   4   5   6   7   8   9   10   Doer

6. What will you do differently as a result of these truths? (please be specific)

LESSON FIVE

"THE PROBLEM OF PLAYING FAVORITES"

James 2:1-13

The Jewish society at the time of Christ was one of the most prejudicial cultures of history. They were extremely separatist with all who were outside the pure faith as they saw it. This included two main categories: the Samaritans, and the Gentiles. The Samaritans were kind of Jewish half-breeds. They were of the region of Samaria and although their roots were Jewish, their practice of their faith had been influenced by other religions and gods. Jews hated Samaritans and had no dealings with them out of fear of being made impure spiritually. If a Jew was traveling from north to south in Israel, he would cross the river Jordan just before Samaria and travel on the other side until he had passed the region. A devout Jew would not even allow his shadow to touch a Samaritan nor would he cross the shadow of a Samaritan. The parable of the "Good Samaritan" was probably pretty hard for many Jews to swallow, for they were so steeped in hatred that they probably thought the only good Samaritan was a dead one.

Devout Jews were even more prejudiced against Gentiles. They viewed all Gentiles as heathens and avoided them. Even if a Gentile wanted to repent of his sins and worship the God of the Jews, he could never be a full Jew. Even if he was circumcised and became fully obedient to the Law in every area, he was still a second-class Jew with even less religious privilege than women. He was not allowed to enter the temple itself, but only the outer porch. A sign over the door warned that Gentiles entered at the risk of their lives. In fact, the Apostle Paul was beaten and imprisoned by the Jews because of false charges that he had taken Gentiles into the temple and thus defiled it.

James' message here in chapter two was especially pointed to the audience of his letter which was Jewish Christians. He is trying to show them that their former prejudices had to be laid aside if they were to hold on to their faith in Christ.

The Principle (2:1)

📖 What is the "big idea" of this verse James uses to begin the chapter?

James is tackling the human tendency to play favorites in our relationships and inconsistently live out the call to love our neighbor. He admonishes, don't try to hold on to your faith in Christ and your prejudices both, because the two don't mix. They work against each other. They are like oil and water – irreconcilable.

📖 Take a moment to try and define in your own words what you believe James means by "*personal favoritism.*"

The Greek word for "*personal favoritism*" used here is positioned at the first of the verse for emphasis. This personal favoritism James speaks of carries the idea of showing preference because of flawed value judgments – those based on externals and appearances. The Greek word is often used negatively of God since He shows no partiality and is not a respecter of persons— e.g. Acts 10:34, Romans 2:11). In fact, The word carries the idea of showing preference because of value judgments based on externals and appearance.

This would be a particular problem to Christians coming from a Jewish background as these were (1:1), for Jewish society was very segregated and highly prejudicial.

📖 Who is James' primary audience, and what effect does that have on interpreting this passage?

By using the term *"brethren"* James clarifies that he is speaking to those who are already believers – not just Jews, but Jewish Christians. This passage (as well as the whole book) is not addressing how to be a believer, but rather, its message is, "since you are a believer, this is how you ought to be living." There is no room in authentic faith for racism and prejudice. They are remnants of our fallenness which must be turned away from.

The Principle in Illustration (2:2-4)

📖 Explain in your own words the circumstances of this example James uses.

In a story reminiscent of the parables told by Jesus, James speaks of two men enter an assembly (literally "Synagogue"). He probably means a gathering for worship. The first appears to be rich and is dressed in flashy clothes with several gold rings. James implies he had rings on every finger and was obviously a person of great wealth. In his culture, rings were an outward sign of wealth and status, and could even be rented for social occasions much like we would rent a tuxedo or limousine. The word for *"fine clothes"* James uses (*lampra* from which our English word "lamp" is derived) is translated "*shining*" in Acts 10:30, and has the idea of bright, flashy clothes, a rare luxury in a society accustomed to brown and grey cloth.

The other person James mentions appears to be poor and is wearing dirty (literally "vile") clothes. One could say that the only ring he has is around his collar. In any culture the contrast would be pronounced and the tendency to favor one over the other would be a common temptation.

📖 What is the reaction given to each of the men and why?

The central character seems to be an usher, and he shows preferential treatment to the one wearing the fine clothes based on his first impression. Apparently he is operating on the "Golden Rule" (the one with all the gold gets to make the rules). The reaction to the other man is quite the opposite.

📖 What criteria does the individual use for determining his treatment of each of the men?

The snap value judgement by the usher was made purely on the basis of externals (i.e. Gold rings and fine clothes verses dirty clothes) rather than spiritual qualities (i.e. humility, obedience, and faith) - the way God views us. "*Man looks at the outward appearance, but the Lord looks at the heart*" (1 Samuel 16:7).

📖 What is the resulting treatment given to each man?

The one who appears to be rich is afforded special attention and given a good place to sit. The apparently poor man can sit on the floor or out of the way. Notice his statement: *"you stand over there, or sit down by my footstool."* The narrative implies that the usher has both a seat and a footstool, and yet he is unwilling to give up either to the poor man.

📖 What is the underlying motive in the judgments made?

James' verdict is that the usher and those like him have "become judges with evil motives." The person was operating on his own value system, not God's. He was giving special treatment to the one who could offer him something in return. Presumably, the wealthy man could contribute more when the collection plate was passed.

The Principle in Evaluation (2:5-11)

📖 According to James, why was this practice wrong?

The person James singles out as a negative illustration is not wrong because he treats the rich man well, but because he doesn't treat them both equally. He dishonored the poor man whom God values and honors (see 1:9,27; 2:5). James viewed this as very important. The Apostle Paul brings up in Galatians 2:9-10 that to *"remember the poor"* was a direct instruction he and Barnabas received from James at the Jerusalem Council (see Acts 15).

📖 How does James clarify in verse 5 that this practice would be incompatible with the Lord?

James begins with a command to *"Listen."* When he references the *"poor"* he uses a term in Greek that literally means "crouched," having the idea of one who humble. James is saying that God has blessed the poor (or humble) with richness of faith. He probably has in view the Sermon on the Mount (Matthew 5:3) where Jesus said, *"Blessed are the poor in spirit, for theirs is the kingdom of heaven."*

Some other reasons for honoring the poor man are:
- God is not partial (Acts 10:34, Rom.2:11)
- God honors the poor (1:27, 2:5, Gal.2:10)
- God doesn't favor riches but rather, poverty of spirit (Psalm 51:16-17, 1 Samuel 15:22)

The favoritism shown here is wrong because it inverts the proper value system. God considers a man rich because of his faith and his position in the kingdom, not gold (which will be used for asphalt in heaven).

📖 Based on what James says in verses 6 and 7, is the favoritism shown a logical response?

James makes it clear here that the response he condemns doesn't even make sense when you take the time to analyze it. The rich of his day usually got that way by taking advantage of others and by oppression. It is unusual to find someone who gets rich by looking out for the interests of others first. The lifestyles of most of the wealthy in the first century blasphemed the name of God (see also Romans 2:24) so it wasn't even logical to be honoring them.

📖 Compare and contrast verses 4 and 8. What is the real problem?

James clarifies his point here by making it clear that loving and honoring the rich man isn't wrong if it is out of wanting to please God. Even if the special treatment of the wealthy was from good motives, that still doesn't make up for dishonoring the poor man any more than stopping at three previous stop signs will convince a policeman to let you off for running one. The root problem is "selective obedience" - following God only when it is personally profitable, which isn't really following God's will but our own. Loving the rich man does not make up for not loving the poor man.

📖 Verse 9 identifies this response as sin. Which action is sin - honoring the rich man or dishonoring the poor man and why?

Both actions are wrong according to James. Even doing the right things can be sin if done for the wrong motives. Honoring the rich man was wrong because his motives were evil (2:4). Dishonoring the poor man was sin because it went against God's will (2:5)

📖 What do verses 10 and 11 teach us about the character of the law?

Verses 10 and 11 make two important points: First, the law operates as a unit (sort of like a fence) and when we break one law It is like a fence with a hole it it. It doesn't matter how solid the rest of the fence is - if there is one hole the cows can get out. Second, in God's economy only a perfect score passes.

📖 According to verses 10 and 11, are there varying degrees of guilt?

It is clear from this passage that there aren't different degrees of guilt. Some actions may have greater earthly consequences than others, but before God, if you stumble at one point you are guilty of all the law — either you are a sinner or you aren't (Romans chapter 3 makes it clear that all have sinned). There is no such thing as a "good sinner" or a "bad sinner." Sin is sin. The only solution is to be judged by a different law — "*the law of liberty*" (2:12).

The Principle in Application (2:12-13)

📖 What effect should the fact that we will be judged by the "*law of liberty*" have on our judging of others?

Since God gives us grace instead of justice, then for us to expect justice in our dealings with others is abhorrent to God (See Matthew

18:21-35). Since God's wisdom is *"full of mercy"* (3:17), then following His wisdom should reflect this in our dealing with others.

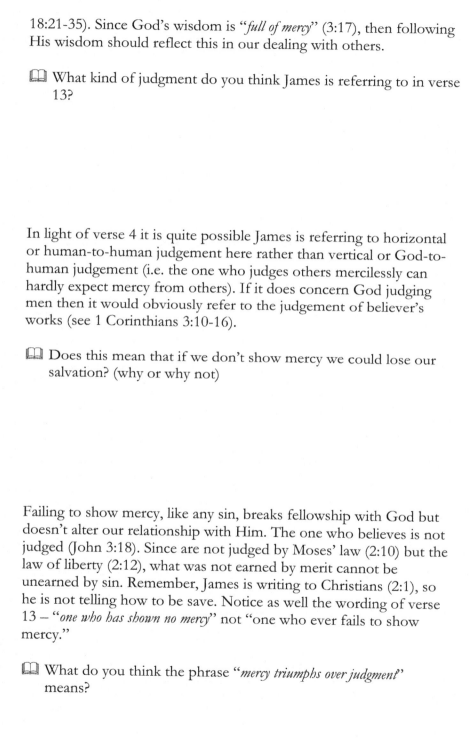 What kind of judgment do you think James is referring to in verse 13?

In light of verse 4 it is quite possible James is referring to horizontal or human-to-human judgement here rather than vertical or God-to-human judgement (i.e. the one who judges others mercilessly can hardly expect mercy from others). If it does concern God judging men then it would obviously refer to the judgement of believer's works (see 1 Corinthians 3:10-16).

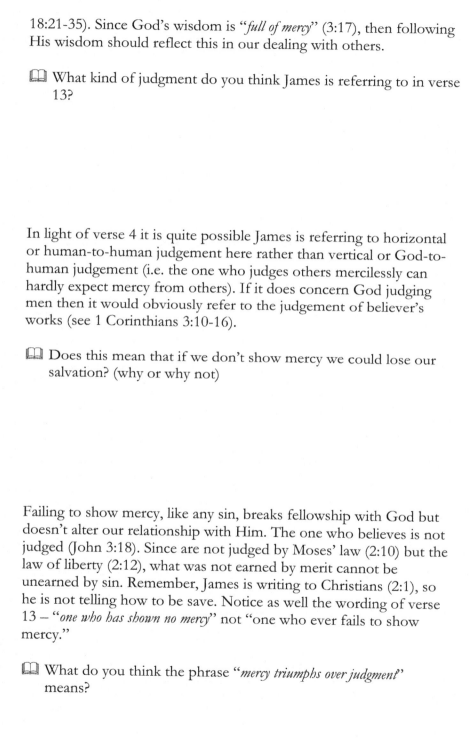 Does this mean that if we don't show mercy we could lose our salvation? (why or why not)

Failing to show mercy, like any sin, breaks fellowship with God but doesn't alter our relationship with Him. The one who believes is not judged (John 3:18). Since are not judged by Moses' law (2:10) but the law of liberty (2:12), what was not earned by merit cannot be unearned by sin. Remember, James is writing to Christians (2:1), so he is not telling how to be save. Notice as well the wording of verse 13 – *"one who has shown no mercy"* not "one who ever fails to show mercy."

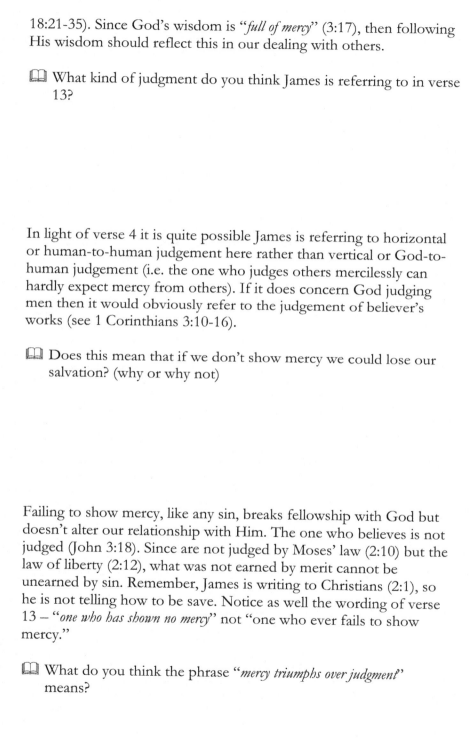 What do you think the phrase *"mercy triumphs over judgment"* means?

James' wording here is a bit challenging to understand. The phrase may mean God's grace or mercy conquers our deserved judgement for sin. But it may also have the idea of mercy when used in our relationships with others accomplishes what judgement cannot do.

📖 What should be our standard in judging others?

James will address this challenging problem more fully a little later in the book. In 4:11-12 he states, *"Do not speak against one another, brethren. He who speaks against a brother or judges a brother, speaks against the law and judges the law; but if you judge the law, you are not a doer of the law but a judge of it. There is only one Lawgiver and Judge, the One who is able to save and to destroy; but who are you who judge your neighbor?"* Our standard in judging others should be the way we ourselves are judged by God (Mercy).

📖 What should be our motive?

The motive for our dealings with others should be love and the Royal Law (2:8) rather than selfishness (2:4). That is one of the works Christ wants to accomplish as we walk with Him.

Personal Application

God's final purpose in our lives is to conform us to the image of Christ (Romans 8:29). If Christ is God (and He is), and God is not partial (and He isn't), then for us to show partiality in our relationships with believers or non-believers is to miss the mark (sin). God used a vision from Heaven to shake Peter from the partiality of his culture (Acts 10:9-35). He desires as well to shake us from the partiality of our culture. The following is to aid in this process.

1. The example James selected involved partiality on the basis of wealth. These are some other criteria that often lead to unbiblical distinctions. Circle the one you are guilty of:

a) Education   d) Looks   g) Spirituality

b) Personality   e) Race   h) Talents

c) Age   f) Position   i) _____

2. How would you rate yourself at relating to those who are different or have nothing to offer you?

NEED IMPROVEMENT 1 2 3 4 5 6 7 8 9 10 GOOD

3. What specific changes need to be made in your attitudes/actions as a result of these truths?

LESSON SIX

"A FAITH THAT WORKS"

James 2:10-26

One of the most common misunderstandings one encounters in explaining the gospel to unbelievers is the 'scales mentality'. This is the idea that when we stand before God, He will place our good works on one side of the scale and our bad on the other. If our good outweighs our bad then we're allowed into heaven. Although this thinking seems to make sense at a glance, at the root of it is a totally illogical premise, namely, that a good deed can make up for a bad. Consider this principle in application. This logic would be like telling a policeman who had pulled you over for running a stop sign that you had stopped at it yesterday, or that you will stop at it tomorrow. You see, stopping at a stop sign a hundred times doesn't take away the guilt of not stopping at it one time. He would still write you a ticket. Consider an even more outrageous example: this perverted logic would allow a murderer to atone for his actions simply by making two choices not to murder. You see, when we do what is right, we are only doing what God requires of us. He gives us no extra credit for it. No parent is going to let his child off from a spanking for disobedience simply because he balances it with an act of obedience, for obedience is expected.

Consider this analogy: Getting to heaven by doing good deeds alone is like trying to swim the Atlantic Ocean. One swimmer might drown after half a mile, another might make it two miles, and yet another, an Olympic athlete, might make it for ten or twenty miles. But how far each person makes it is irrelevant, for none of them could possibly make it far enough. The distance between man and God is too great for man to cross, for God is perfect, and no matter how good man is, he is always imperfect. He may be better than any other man, but he is still imperfect. The ancient Greek word for "sin" (*hamartano*) was an archery term, and meant 'to miss the mark', and the mark God calls us to hit is His glory which is manifested in Christ. When God pulls out the scales of justice, He doesn't weigh our good deeds against our bad, or weigh us against our fellowman, but He places us on one side of the scale and Christ on the other. By this standard it is easy to see why all fall short or 'miss the mark'. That's why all are called sinners, and why works without faith is not enough.

In this passage James clarifies the fact that works without faith equals nothing in God's eyes. Let's look at it.

Works Without Faith Equals Nothing (2:10-13)

📖 What problems does James present in these verses?

As we looked at briefly last week, the Mosaic law operates as a unit – it is all inclusive. The problem with this is that only a perfect score passes. Since everyone will stumble at some point and according to verse 10 become "guilty of all", then all are convicted by the Law as guilty and transgressors (2:9). As the Apostle Paul stated in Romans 3:23, "For all have sinned and fall short of the glory of God." While at a human level, we like to grade on a scale of good to bad sinners, God sees us as either guilty or not.

📖 Does he give a clear solution and if so, what?

Our only hope, since we are guilty under the Mosaic law, is to be judged by a different standard – the law of liberty. James will elaborate more on this concept of grace in the rest of his book.

📖 James apparently refers to two types of "law" (see 2:10, 11, 12). What are the differences or distinctions between them?

The Mosaic law is a law of rules and standards that have no power to change man because they operate externally. It merely reveals our sin. The law of liberty is a law of grace which, because it operates internally, facilitates change as a response to forgiveness.

📖 According to this passage, do you believe it is possible for a person to be saved by works (apart from faith in Christ)? (explain your answer)

No, it is not possible for anyone to be saved by good works independent of Christ. Only one who fulfills the law perfectly could be saved by the law and the only person who could and did do that is God revealed in His son Jesus Christ. Because "all have sinned" (Romans 3:23) and because that makes us guilty of the whole law (see 2:10), no one can be saved apart from faith in Christ.

📖 Compare verse 13 with Matthew 5:7; 6:14; and 7:1.

This comparison is not meant to reveal new truth, but rather to show the link between James' epistle and the "Sermon on the Mount". Even though he probably wasn't a believer yet, this message of Christ's obviously had a great impact on James since his entire epistle is filled with references to it.

Faith Without Works Equals Nothing (2:14-20)

📖 Is James contrasting true faith with dead works (as Paul does), or true faith with dead faith? (explain your answer)

Here in verse 14 James begins with a hypothetical question: "What use is it" (literally, "What is the profit") to say you have faith and not back it up with works? James is not (as many have implied) contrasting faith and works in this passage, but rather, two kinds of faith – true or authentic faith which reveals itself by good works, and counterfeit faith which gives verbal assent yet has no works to give evidence of its reality.

📖 Is faith without works "saving faith"? (compare 2:14-17 with Titus 1:16)

No, faith which is verbally claimed yet unaccompanied by any works is not a faith which can save. The question in verse 14, "can that faith same him?" is rhetorical with a negative answer implied in verses 15 and 16 and spelled out in verse 17.

📖 Does this passage advocate "witnessing with your life" instead of verbal, initiative evangelism? (explain your answer)

No, this passage should not be taken to overemphasize actions to the exclusion of communicating our faith verbally. Even though it isn't enough just to "say" we have faith, we still need to be sure we don't neglect going public with our faith. Romans 10:9-10 makes it clear that we must "confess" Christ with our mouths, not just believe in our hearts.

📖 Does true faith include words, works or both?

True, saving faith includes both words and works. Verse 12 directs us to, "...so speak and so act..." Words clarify the source of our works. Works give our words meaning. We should say it, but those around us should also see it. James explains his perspective with two illustrations. The first is that of a Christian who is needy. A fellow Christian greets them but does not help them: "Go in peace, be warmed and be filled." This verbal blessing is a sort of wish. In our day we might say "I hope you get clothed and fed." James' conclusion is that words are not enough. This passage should not be construed as saying that words of blessing and encouragement are unimportant, but rather that they are not enough by themselves. The point of James' illustration is that if I say I want them to be clothed and fed, but I do not do what I can to see that happen, then one must conclude that I really don't mean what I say. Verse 17 points out that in the same way, faith that is without works is not living faith but dead faith.

📖 How is verse 18 a more logical statement than verse 14?

The situation James alludes to is: person A claims to have faith but they have no works, person B says "I have works", implying that they are a demonstration of the fact that they have faith ("I will show you my faith..."). The logical question an outsider must ask is "how can faith be demonstrated without works?" Faith and it's fruit (works) belong together just as apples belong on an apple tree. The only reason an apple tree doesn't produce apples is if it is dead or else it isn't really an apple tree. The only reason real faith (the theme of the book of James) does not result in works is if it isn't **really saving faith**. Just as fruit is the logical proof of a fruit tree, works are the logical proof of faith.

📖 What effect does verse 19 have on the argument that belief is enough?

What are the ramifications of this idea?

It is not enough to give intellectual assent to Christ, nor is it enough to have an emotional experience. Even demons "believe" in God and at least it has an impact on them emotionally (they shudder or tremble), but they aren't going to heaven. True, saving faith must also include the activation of our wills. In light of 1:21-27 knowledge only benefits us as we act on it. If we really believe we will live our lives accordingly. If we don't act on our beliefs, we don't really believe them.

📖 Is James saying we are saved by works? (Tell what verses you base your conclusion on and why.)

James is saying we are saved by faith alone but not by a faith that is alone (has no works). In James 2:1 he speaks of our faith in Christ, not our works. Later in 2:18 he doesn't say "my works save me", only that his faith is shown by his works. The issue isn't that faith saves, but what kind of faith saves. True saving faith is "a faith that works".

James says, "You believe that God is one," The phrase "God is one" comes from what is known as the "Shema", Judaism's basic confession of faith. It comes from Deuteronomy 6:4 which says "Hear, O Israel! The Lord our God, the Lord is One!" "Shema" is Hebrew for the first word, "hear." According to rabbinical law, it was to be recited morning and night. It was the foundational doctrine of a Jew, and one could not be a Jew without giving verbal assent to this belief. The Jews prided themselves in this belief, and with one statement James shows how little value that has toward salvation: His point seems to be, "So what! Even the demons (which certainly aren't saved) believe that, and at least it has some result in them (they shudder in fear)." James' conclusion is wrapped up in verse 20: "faith without works is useless" (literally, "dead").

Faith That Works Equals Justification (2:21-26)

📖 Doesn't verse 21 seem to imply salvation by works? How does this affect your interpretation of this passage?

Yes, one must recognize that verse 21 does seem to imply salvation by works, but since that would contradict the teaching of numerous other passages, that is obviously not what James is saying. Part of the confusion here stems from the term "justified". When Paul uses the term in Romans he means "to declare a sinner righteous" and equates it with salvation. When James uses the term here he means "to vindicate" or "to prove to be righteous." He would agree with Paul that a sinner is declared or reckoned righteous when he places his faith in God (see 2:23).

Paul begins this treatise on saving faith that produces works by using Abraham as an illustration. In the mind of a Jew (and James' audience is "the twelve tribes scattered abroad" or Jewish Christians), there is none greater than Abraham. You see this evidenced in the title, "our father." To a Jew, if anyone makes it into heaven, it will be Abraham.

📖 When was Abraham "reckoned righteous"? What Old Testament passage was this quoted from (see cross references if your Bible has them)?

Abraham was "reckoned righteous" when he believed God (exhibited faith). This quote comes from Genesis 15:6 and follows God's promise to give Abraham a son and descendants as numerous as the stars of the heavens. James states, "The Scripture was fulfilled"; when Abraham offered up Isaac, he fulfilled what was said of him: "He believed God and it was counted to him as righteousness." The Greek word here for "believed" is the verb form of the word for "faith". When Abraham believed, he was credited with righteousness. The emphasis here must be on the fact that God is the one declaring Abraham righteous, for there is none higher than He to overturn such a verdict.

It is essential that we get a handle on the exact meaning of this word "justified" as it appears here. By not doing so, many have drawn wrong conclusions about what James is saying. The fact that we are not "saved" by works is made crystal clear elsewhere (Ephesians 2:8-9, Romans 3:20), so obviously that is not what James is saying, even though it appears that way at a glance. The Greek word here is *dikaioo*, and shares the same root as the word translated "righteousness" in v.23. The key difference is the ending (*"oo"*). Verbs which end this way generally mean "to bring out that which a person is." We see that definition demonstrated in how this same form is translated elsewhere: Matthew 11:19, Luke 7:35 – "vindicated", 1 Corinthians 4:4 – "acquitted", and especially in Romans 3:4 where it is translated "found." Paul says there, "...let God be found true, though every man be found a liar." Certainly God was already true, but the word emphasizes His being seen to be so. Abraham was "justified" by works in the sense that his works "vindicated" his faith, or proved it to be genuine to others (not to God since God already drew this conclusion years before).

📖 Did this "crediting" with righteousness occur before or after the actions of verse 21, and how does this affect the interpretation?

The key point here is that Abraham was "declared" righteous in Genesis 15:6. It was at that point that God said "Abraham is righteous." When he offered up Isaac (Genesis 22:9-12, many years later) he was proving that what God had already said was true. Abraham was declared righteous by faith alone. Later, by his works, he demonstrated the reality of that faith. At that point, his "faith was perfected." The Greek word "perfected" here shares the same root word as perfect in James 1:4, with the difference being the ending (*"oo"*, see above). The word perfect means: "complete, full-grown, mature." Abraham was "reckoned righteous" thirty years or more before the actions of verse 21 by which he was "justified by works." Therefore, since he was already righteous for 30 years, his works didn't save him; they merely proved the reality of his Genesis 15 faith.

📖 What was the source of Abraham's works (verse 23)?

According to James, the source of Abraham's works was his intimate friendship with God ("and he was called the friend of God"). The more intimately we know God the easier it will be for us to trust Him. The more we trust Him, the more works we will give as evidence of that.

📖 How can you reconcile verse 24 with the Pauline doctrine of justification by faith (Romans 3:28)?

As was mentioned earlier, James is using the term justification differently than Paul. Without a doubt Paul is true in saying "by grace you have been saved through faith...not as a result of works" (Ephesians 2:8,9). But Paul continues in Ephesians 2:10 by saying that we are "created...for good works." James is not refuting the Pauline doctrine of justification by true faith but a perversion of it. James and Paul are not enemies at war with one another, but rather, fellow-soldiers, fighting back-to-back against enemies coming from opposite directions. Paul is contrasting living faith with dead works, while James is contrasting living faith with dead faith. James teaches that we are saved by faith alone, but not a faith that is alone. If ours truly is saving faith, our faith will bear fruit in works. You can't turn a pine tree into a peach tree by hanging peaches on it, but if a peach tree really is a peach tree, it will result in peaches.

📖 What does Abraham the "Father of Israel" have in common with the prostitute Rahab?

What does this say about faith and works?

The selection of Abraham and Rahab as examples is a very unlikely pairing. To the Jew who would read this Abraham would be the best possible example. If anyone made it to heaven Abraham did. He was the "friend of God." In stark contrast to Abraham, Rahab would paint a very different picture in the minds of the Jewish audience of this letter. She had several major strikes against her. First, she wasn't a Jew. Second, she wasn't moral (she was a prostitute). So far as Scripture records it, the only act of faith she ever performed was to hide the spies. When Rahab hid the twelve spies of Canaan (Joshua 2:1-15) instead of reporting them to the city officials, this gave proof that she not only believed that the God of Israel was true, but that she placed her trust in Him. Later, when the city is destroyed, God makes sure that she is spared. James selects her to illustrate his principle of faith being proven by works. As we explained earlier, James uses the word justified here to mean "vindicated" or "proven." The implication is, of course, that it is assumed Rahab had faith. This immoral Gentile had to be viewed by the Jewish Christians as a convert, for she creeps up, of all places, in the genealogy of Christ, listed as the great-grandmother of King David (Matthew 1:5).

Clearly this is a "Greatest to Least" illustration. In the mind of a Jew, Rahab was one of the most doubtful to wind up in heaven. The point of James' contrast seems to be that it doesn't matter how much

75

works our faith produces, but simply that **our faith does produce works**. Abraham and Rahab demonstrated by their actions that they both had faith in God. There is no greater evidence of what we really believe than how we behave. Conversely, if what we say we believe does not affect our behavior it is to be doubted.

📖 Explain in your own words the relationship between faith and works.

In the same way that a body without a spirit equals a dead body, James shows that faith without any works at all equals a dead faith. The bottom line is this: We are saved by faith alone, but not by faith that is alone.

Personal Application

Without a doubt Paul is true in saying *"By grace you have been saved through faith... not as a result of works that no one should boast"*(Ephesians 2:8,9). But he continues in verse 10 by saying that we are *"created in Christ Jesus for good works, which God prepared beforehand, that we should walk in them."* James is not refuting the Pauline doctrine of justification by true faith but a perversion of it. The real issue is not that "faith saves" but "what kind of faith saves?" True Biblical faith is "a faith that works."

1. Have you placed your faith in Jesus? If not, why not? (be honest)

2. If yes, what changes have resulted from that decision?

3. What is there in your life that can only be explained by your faith in Jesus?

4. How are you doing at cultivating a growing friendship (2:23) with God? (please circle where you are now)

Casual   Friend
Acquaintance 1 2 3 4 5 6 7 8 9 10 of God

How to Grow a Tree that Bears Fruit

1. Plant the seed (If you have not yet trusted Christ do so).

2. Care for the root (Water it with God's Word and cultivate it with prayer).

3. Care for the fruit (Pick it when it's ripe—be obedient to what God calls you to do).

4. Prune it (Be willing to let go of things that hinder your fruitfulness).

5. Wait (There is not substitute for time – younger Christians should not be frustrated if they bear less fruit than older, more mature Christians).

LESSON SEVEN

"TACKLING THE TONGUE"
James 3:1-12

The sign, "Slippery When Wet", definitely applies to the tongue, and since the tongue is always wet, it allows for some great slip-ups. The ads below actually appeared in newspaper adds or classifieds.

SNAKE FOR SALE - Eats anything and is fond of children

LOST: Small, apricot poodle. Reward. Neutered Like one of the family.

WANTED: Man to take care of cow that does not smoke or drink

We do not tear your clothing with machinery. We do it carefully by hand

FOR SALE: Antique desk suitable for lady with thick legs and large drawers

3 YEAR OLD teacher needed for pre-school, experience preferred

WANTED: Hair-cutter. Excellent growth potential

Stock up and save. Limit: one

Mixing bowl set designed to please a cook with round bottom for sufficient beating

USED CARS: Why go elsewhere to be cheated? Come here first!

We are going to look at James' admonitions on the tongue in James

3:1-12. As we do, you may be tempted to "bite your tongue" a few times, but realize that it is capable of doing some biting of it's own.

Introduction (3:1-2)

📖 In light of chapters 1 and 2, and in light of his audience, what is the significance of the warning in verse 1?

In light of the fact that we are accountable to be doers and not just hearers, it would be a grave sin for a teacher to instruct others to do what he himself does not do. In 2:14 James warns against saying what you do not show. In 2:12 he says "so speak and so act as those who are to be judged by the law of liberty". This would especially apply to teachers since their teaching, if wrong, would lead many astray of this. Since they are Jews separated from the Mother Church, there was probably a shortage of qualified teachers and thus a real temptation for those who aren't qualified to try to teach because of the prestige of the office. These would need to be warned of the seriousness of teaching others.

📖 In light of this context why does he warn against becoming teachers?

Since the tongue is the "tool of the trade" for a teacher there will be many more opportunities to stumble in what he or she says. Because of the position of instructor, this stumbling would impact far more lives than just his own. James uses the first-person plural because he himself is a teacher in the church and knows that he must some day give account to the divine Judge for his teaching.

📖 What do you think is involved in the "stricter judgment" James speaks of?

Since James is writing to Christians (2:1), the judgment spoken of would not be directed toward salvation, but rather, toward the judgment of the believer's works and the giving of reward (1 Corinthians 3:10-16). may have in mind the "Bema" judgement of believer's works (I Cor. 3:10-16), but more likely refers to the fact that, It also may have in view the fact that because of his prominent position, a teacher's life will be scrutinized much more closely than it otherwise would be.

📖 What explanation does he give for his warning (see verse 2)?

We already saw in 1:26 that "If anyone thinks himself to be religious, and yet does not bridle his tongue but deceives his own heart, this man's religion is worthless." We all stumble in many ways and stumbles of speech are the last to be mastered. As someone once said, "Life is strewn with banana peels." The word "stumble" is in the present tense, meaning we continuously stumble. The one who does not stumble in speech is said to be "perfect." The Greek word here (*teleios*) does not mean without flaw, but rather, has the idea of "mature, or full grown." In other words, a tongue that is under control is an evidence of maturity.

📖 Identify all the ways the tongue is identified in verses 1-12.

A horse's mouth (ha!), a ship's rudder, a fire, a world of iniquity, a restless evil, full of deadly poison, untamable.

The Prominence of the Tongue (3:3-5)

📖 Identify the three illustrations James gives of the tongue's prominence.

How are they similar?

How are they different?

It is a bit humorous that James' first analogy of the tongue is a horse's mouth. Actually, the tongue in this comparison refers to the bit in a horse's mouth which directs its entire body. The second illustration is a ship's rudder, which directs the entire ship. Last, James compares the tongue to a small fire which sets aflame a great forest. Each, though it is small, has a very great impact – much larger than itself. Some have a positive result while others have a negative one.

There are two which yield a positive result (bit and rudder). In order for the bit to be effective at directing the horse, it must be held in check by the hands of another. Often this directing will run contrary to the tendency of the horse. We'll explore this further in a moment. Like the horse, the ship is large, and yet able to be directed by a very small piece of wood: the rudder. Like the bit, the key to the rudder's effectiveness is being in the hands of another. Also, the directing of the pilot counters the driving force of the wind. In these first two illustrations we glean an important fact about our own tongues. They must be guided and controlled by placing them in the hands of another — Jesus. The negative example also makes an important point. James picks up the theme of the smallness of the tongue, yet its great effect. An entire forest can be set aflame by one small spark.

So, James gives us three illustrations, two of which are positive, and one which is negative. Taken together, another significant point emerges, for in the same way, the tongue has a great potential for positive use AND for great destruction if not controlled.

📖 How do these comparisons affect the significance of this passage?

Here in verse 5, James clarifies the common denominator that all three illustrations share with the statement: "So also the tongue is a small part of the body, and yet it boasts of great things." These illustrations show how important and significant this area is. There are 108 verses in the book of James and there are over 60 references to speaking. Obviously this is an area James is quite concerned with.

The Product of the Tongue (3:6-8)

Perhaps no political relationship has garnered more attention in modern times than the one between Sir Winston Churchill and his political rival Lady Astor. Their antics were infamous throughout the British Isles. On one particular occasion the two were at a party and wound up taking the same elevator as they left. As the elevator began its decent, Lady Astor turned and said, "Sir Churchill, I perceive that you are drunk!", to which the quick-witted Churchill replied, "Yes I am, and you, Lady Astor, are ugly". And with a final jab he added, "And tomorrow I will be sober". On another occasion the two found themselves across the table from one another in a political discussion. At an appropriate juncture Lady Astor took advantage of having Churchill captive and declared, "Sir Churchill, if you were my husband I'd put arsenic in your tea!", to which Churchill retorted, "Lady Astor, if you were my wife, I'd drink it!" Although these two don't serve as good role models of godly use of the tongue, they do illustrate how easy it is to use our tongue to damage another.

📖 What insights can you draw from the tongue being called a fire?

Fire has a tremendous potential for good (heat, light, cooking, etc.) or for destruction. James says the tongue "...sets on fire the course of our life" – (Lit. "the wheel of nature"). It is only constructive as it is used wisely. Although specific applications may be drawn, the word "our" does not appear in the original text. Its main intent is more general (i.e. the tongue's destructive effects have impacted the whole course of human existence).

📖 What do you think the phrase "world of iniquity" means here?

The Greek word for "world" here (*cosmos*) has the idea of the space something takes up, or the arena in which something operates. Here James indicates that the tongue is the arena where iniquity (Lit. "injustice") thrives. In a very tangible way the tongue is the "Mouthpiece of Sin". It operates in the realm of iniquity because it is directly linked to the heart - the source of our sin problem. We will look more fully at this aspect in a moment.

📖 Compare and contrast verse 6 with Matthew 15:11 and identify that verse's context and its impact on the overall meaning.

Humanity's problems with the tongue are internal not external. The Pharisees were concerned with external cleanliness which had no effect on the real problem – our evil hearts.

📖 What does verse 6 imply about the source of our problems with the tongue?

It is "set on fire by hell". The implication is that Satan is somehow involved in our problems with the tongue. The stumblings of our speech are a direct result of our fallenness, which can be traced back to Satan's success in the Garden with tempting Adam and Eve to go their own way independent of God.

📖 According to verses 7 and 8 can the tongue be tamed?

Not only does James say all animals are tamable, but also that all types have been tamed at one point. This makes it doubly hard to understand why the tongue is untamable. Yet James makes that point emphatically. This phrase literally reads, "But the tongue no one to tame is able of men." This is significant, for the Greek word for men (*anthropon*) is not necessary unless it is there as a clarifier, to leave room for the fact that God is able to tame the tongue. In other words, absolutely no one from the realm of man is able to tame the tongue (but with God nothing is impossible).

📖 Do you ever find yourself trying to tame your tongue?

Sermons are frequently preached on this passage with the title normally being, "Taming the Tongue", and the focus being on "watching what we say", a futile exercise in light of verse 8. James' point is that it is impossible for humans to tame the tongue.

📖 Compare and contrast verse 8 with Matthew 12:30-37. According to this, what is the only way to change our speech?

No one can tame the tongue because it will always speak "out of that which fills the heart". The reason the tongue is untamable is because it is connected to the heart. The only way to change the tongue is to change the heart, which fortunately God is able to do (Ps.51:10). The key, as in the illustrations of vs. 3-5, is to have someone else in control (God).

📖 Have you experienced the "deadly poison" of the tongue?

Have you been guilty of using it on others?

James closes verse 8 by saying the tongue is full of "deadly poison." It is important to remember that death, Biblically speaking, does not mean cessation, but separation. The poison of the tongue is "death bearing: in that when it is out of God's control, it separates people, rather that creating the unity God desires.

The Practice of the Tongue (3:9-12)

📖 In what way is the tongue inconsistent?

With it we "bless God", yet with the same tongue we curse man who is God's creation and bears His image. The term "curse" here (*kataraomai*) isn't talking about profanity or four-letter words. It has the idea of wishing evil on someone. From James' lips we are admonished, "My brethren, these things ought not to be this way".

📖 What is so wrong about the inconsistency in verses 9 and 10?

To curse man is to curse God who created him. This inconsistent action is a reflection of the double-mindedness James speaks of in 1:8 and 4:8 which is abhorrent to God.

📖 Compare this passage with James 1:26.

Our unbridled tongue is an evidence of a deceived heart and a worthless faith. Not dealing with our hearts enslaves us to the Pharisaical practices of legalism, modifying behavior while failing to deal with the wrong attitudes of our heart. Such approaches will not succeed for self-will has no power to master sin. If we could conquer by our own self-effort, we wouldn't need a savior.

📖 What does the consistency of creation in the examples James mentions here have to do with our own inconsistency?

These three fruits James mentions (fig, olive, and grapes), found in all the Near East, are particularly associated with Palestine. His audience would have been quite familiar as well. Even at it's widest point, Israel is always close to salt water in the form of the ocean or the Dead Sea, so even in James' time of limited travel, most everyone could journey to the sea. James uses the consistencies of creation to spotlight and condemn our own inconsistency.

📖 If the heart is the tree whose fruit the tongue bears, what does your speech reveal about your heart?

Personal Application

In chapter one James exhorted us to prove ourselves *"doers of the Word, and not merely hearers who delude themselves"* (1:22). In doing that with this passage it is essential to trace the problem to its root. In Matthew 12:34 Christ said, *"the mouth speaks out of that which fills the heart."* This is the reason James says *"no one can tame the tongue."* The tongue will always speak *"out of that which fills the heart,"* so the only way to change our speech is to change our hearts. Fortunately, for us, God is in the business of changing hearts. The following is to help you make your heart available for God's working.

1. "Sticks and stones may break my bones but words will never hurt me." How true is this in your experience?

2. Can you recall a time when someone's words were helpful? What did they say?

3. Can you recall a time when someone's words were harmful? What did they say?

4. Can you think of some recent examples when you have done either 2 or 3?

5. How consistent is your speech?

Very Consistent 1 2 3 4 5 6 7 8 9 10 Very Inconsistent

6. Do you tend more to try to tame your tongue or do you let it show you what is in your heart?

7. What do you need to be doing differently?

8. King David prayed "create in me a clean heart, oh God" (Ps.51:10). If that expresses your desire then why not begin today asking God to do that in your life?

LESSON EIGHT

"IN WHO'S EYES, WISE?"

James 3:13-18

In verses 3:1-12 James describes the tongue as uncontrollable, a destructive fire, untamable, a deadly poison. But why? What is it about this symmetrical, very mobile, muscular, unpaired organ situated in the mouth that makes it so dangerous and so worthy of James' attention. Well, perhaps one additional bit of information will shed some light on it. Have you ever been asked by your doctor to "stick out your tongue"? The reason he asks this is because some symptomatic diseases of the human body can be detected by certain alterations of the tongue. Such health issues as allergies, pellagra, sprue, pernacious anemia, and iron and vitamin deficiencies can be diagnosed in such a way. In some cases examination of the tongue can reveal matters as serious as a stroke or even a brain tumor. I believe what James is saying in chapter 3 is the same point. Just as the tongue is able to reveal inward physical disease and serve as a diagnostic tool, so too, in the spiritual realm the tongue can be used as a spiritual diagnosis to reveal what is inside. What can be seen on the outside reveals what is going on on the inside. What is on the heart eventually ends up on the lips. There are two solutions to our problems with the tongue. Either we can cut it out, in which case it is no longer able to do damage (or good for that matter), or we can learn the lesson of James chapter 3. Verses 13-18 are an application of verses 1-12. Lets take a look.

The Call to Wisdom (3:13)

📖 Compare and contrast verse 13 with Proverbs 9:10.

Solomon advises us that "The fear of the Lord is the beginning of wisdom, and the knowledge of the Holy One is understanding." The obvious implication is that true wisdom and understanding are only found through rightly relating to God. One who doesn't fear God cannot show good deeds in gentleness.

📖 Define "wise" (see also Colossians 1:9, 10) and "understanding" in your own words, and describe their parameters as you understand them.

The Greek word translated "wisdom" here (*sophos*) is probably derived from the Hebrew word "*sophim*" signifying watchmen. It had the idea in Greek culture of ascending a high mountaintop to gain a vantage point from which to determine a course of action. Its basic meaning is one who knows how to regulate his life based on what he sees. When applied to believers it has the idea of practical and spiritual insight, especially of a moral nature. Understanding (*epistamai*) has more of an idea of intellectual insight, knowledge, to know well.

📖 In light of this passage, how are these two demonstrated?

Wisdom and understanding, James instructs us, are demonstrated by good behavior and by deeds done in gentleness of wisdom. James' point seems to be, "if you have these, prove it." Good behavior literally carries the idea of good "conversation." The Greek word used here for gentle means meekness that is expressed not in a person's outward behavior only nor in his or her relations to othersn or mere natural disposition, but expressed rather as an inwrought grace of the soul, first and chiefly directed toward God. This same word is translated "humility" in James 1:21.

📖 What is the difference between "good behavior" and "deeds in the gentleness of wisdom?"

It seems that "good behavior" has to do with what one does while "deeds done in the gentleness of wisdom" has to do with how one does what he or she does.

📖 Of what significance is this verse's context?

It is significant to note that this exhortation is given in the context of dealing with the tongue. Again, we learned in James 1:26, "If anyone thinks himself to be religious, and yet does not bridle his tongue but deceives his own heart, this man's religion is worthless." Our good behavior must be manifest in our words, and even our deeds sometimes involve speech.

The Contrast of False Wisdom (3:14-16)

James transitions beginning in 3:14 by showcasing a different mindset that the wisdom he calls us toward. He highlights first of all, bitter jealousy (being fearful of the advantage of others). The wording carries the idea of that funny feeling you sometimes get in the pit of your stomach when something good happens to someone else. It can carry the fear of being replaced by someone else as King Saul with David. Next, he mentions selfish ambition (seeking the advantage of self). The Greek word (*eritheia*) is derived from *"erithos"*, one who works for hire, or one whose involvement is motivated by what they get out of it instead of a servant's heart. It seeks to replace others or to get its own way. In 1 Corinthians 3:1-3 Paul makes a similar point.

The fleshly believer is exemplified by jealousy and strife (the same root word as selfish ambition).

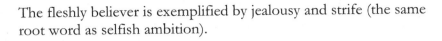 What is the origin of the false wisdom James mentions in verse 15?

"This wisdom is not that which comes down from above", James advises. The root word for "not" here (*ou*) is a stronger negative, and appears as the first word of the sentence in Greek for added emphasis. In other words, if the wisdom operates with jealousy and selfish ambition, it absolutely cannot be from God. This wisdom is not God's but is earthly, natural, and demonic.

What is the significance of the three descriptions given?

The three descriptions link false wisdom directly with the three enemies of the believer – the world (earthly), the flesh (natural), and the devil (demonic). "Earthly" conveys the idea of arising from the earth and attached to it; limited to the realm of the earth. Because of this, the wisdom spoken of is by necessity finite. The word "natural" used here (*psuchike*) carries the idea of that part of man which is common to the animal realm, animalistic. It is closely akin to "fleshly". This type of wisdom James speaks of is bound to the nature of man, and stands in stark contrast to that which is supernatural and of God. James also calls false wisdom "demonic" (literally "demon-like"). It resembles the mindset of demons; it mimics their thinking. Don't underestimate the power of the unseen world. Satan is able to suggest wisdom in line with his will. The opposites of these three would be heavenly instead of earthly, supernatural instead of natural, and godly instead of demonic.

📖 Look back over these verses and summarize how false wisdom operates (3:14, 16).

False wisdom operates by bitter jealousy and selfish ambition, in our hearts, and through arrogance and lies.

📖 What is the outcome of this false wisdom James identifies (3:16)?

This false wisdom James describes here leads to disorder (i.e. confusion and unsettledness, the opposite of things fitting into place) and every evil thing (i.e. pettiness and carnality). A good question to ask is "What evil is there that is not a result of jealousy or selfish ambition (strife)?" When you compare verse 16 with verse 8, you see that the tongue is a restless (disorder) evil (every evil thing), and speaks from this wisdom. First Corinthians 3:3 uses a similar description (jealousy and strife) and gives a name to this lifestyle – fleshly or carnal.

📖 What types of people are likely to live their lives based on this kind of wisdom?

The non-believer doesn't have a choice in the matter. The wisdom of this world, the god of this world and his fleshly nature all flavor his wisdom. The believer who follows his or her own flesh chooses to listen to their own wisdom fueled by these sources instead of listening to the Lord and drawing on His wisdom.

The Character of True Wisdom (3:17-18)

📖 What is the origin of true wisdom according to 3:17?

The origin of true wisdom is "from above", James says. This adjective tells us the source of true wisdom: from above, where God is. In James 1:17 we see that everything good, and only that which is good, is "from above" (the same Greek word), coming from the "Father of lights" who never changes.

📖 How does this wisdom from above operate (3:17)?

The wisdom from above is pure, peaceable, gentle, reasonable, full of mercy and good fruits, unwavering, without hypocrisy. "Pure" refers to an inner quality of cleanness. It does not mean perfection, but rather, sensitivity to anything unclean (morals and motives). God's wisdom is peaceable. It produces right relationships, in contrast to the disorder of verse 16. This wisdom is described as "gentle", having the idea of meekness. The word was used in ancient Greece of a high-spirited horse who was controlled and well trained. It implies power under control. True wisdom is "reasonable", or "willing to yield", conciliatory, willing to give in – the opposite of stubborn.

James goes on to describe God's heavenly wisdom as "full of mercy" (sensitivity to the needs of others, in contrast to the selfishness of man-made wisdom), and "good fruits" – good, benevolent, profitable, useful. It is "unwavering" (literally "without separation, undivided"). It is consistent and impartial. This wisdom from above is "without hypocrisy." It is genuine, without any masks. This aspect is the culmination of all the rest.

These attributes of God's wisdom are in direct contrast to man-made wisdom which is characterized by jealousy and selfish ambition.

📖 What is the significance of wisdom from above being "first, pure"?

The fact that the characteristic of purity is identified as being first indicates a special prominence. The likely reason is that purity is foundational to all the rest. Without being pure the others aren't possible.

📖 Compare verse 17 with Galatians 5:22-23 and write what you observe.

Galatians 5:22-23 gives a more comprehensive listing of what we know as the "fruit of the Spirit" which incorporates many of the characteristics listed here and relates the results of following God's wisdom. It is always affirming to see different Biblical writers conveying the same truth.

📖 Contrast verse 17 with verses 14-16.

Note the stark contrasts: bitter jealousy - reasonable; selfish ambition - peaceable; arrogant - gentle; lie against the truth - pure, without hypocrisy; disorder - unwavering; every evil thing - full of mercy and good fruits.

📖 What, according to James, is the outcome of true wisdom (3:18)?

The end result of true wisdom is righteousness and peace. "The seed whose fruit is righteousness" is probably a reference to 1:21 where James speaks of receiving the word "implanted" which results in our sanctification (salvation from the present power of sin over our lives). The seed of the word is implanted and takes root in our lives when we receive it humbly (1:21) by a request (1:5) of faith (1:6). The resulting fruit is righteousness (3:18) and the peace that is spoken of is most likely peace with God.

📖 Contrast verse 18 with 1:20 and record your observations.

God's word (true wisdom) rooted in our lives bears fruit in righteousness. Conversely, man's anger or emotions which follow false wisdom (see lesson 3) will never achieve God's righteousness.

📖 What type of person is likely to live their life based on this kind of wisdom James advocates?

The believer who chooses to hear God's wisdom and obey it (see chapter one) is the one who conquers trials and allows them to accomplish God's intent.

Personal Application

We all order our lives by wisdom. The real issue is "what kind of wisdom is it?" The doctor says "stick out your tongue" so he can check your physical condition. Likewise, in chapter three James says "stick out your tongue" so he can check out your spiritual condition (3:2,6). Consider the following as you appraise your own spiritual condition.

Some Questions

1. In appraising your own life, what kind of wisdom have you applied to these areas.

(Perhaps you have never yielded these areas to God's control. Now would be a good time.)

2. Which of the two sources of wisdom has the most influence in your life?

3. Do you sincerely desire to change?

Some Answers

To fully understand the two kinds of wisdom you must look at their source. Earthly wisdom is finite. Its source is you and your limited resources. Godly wisdom is infinite. Its source is God, who not only made this Earth, but your life as well. Perhaps the best question is not what but who is in control of your life?

How to be stuck with "Earthly Wisdom": "Each one is tempted when he is carried away and enticed by his own lust." (1:14)

Self-sufficiency: Depending on ourselves, trusting ourselves, believing we can solve our own problems (Boastful, pride of life).

Self-service: Following our own desires and lusts (1:13-21; 2:1-13), seeking our gain rather than what God provides (4:1-5;6 – the lust of the flesh, the lust of the eyes.)

How to get God's wisdom: "Humble yourselves in the presence of the Lord and He will exalt you:" (4:10).

Confess (4:8): Agree with God concerning your sin (if you are unwilling to repent then you should realize your confession isn't of the heart, but is just lip-service).

Submit (4:7): Ask God to again take control of your life and to give you His wisdom (1:5). Draw near to Him (4:8) and listen to His voice instead of your lusts.

LESSON NINE

"WHAT IN THE WORLD DO YOU WANT"
James 4:1-10

America's love affair with things has grown to an obsession. In 1950 roughly 10% of the nation's income was spent on luxuries. By 1980 that figure had grown to 30%. Currently, the wealthiest in America spend about 65% of their income on luxury goods. That is probably in line with what one would expect, but the surprising discovery of a recent study by Torsten Slok, chief international economist for Deutsche Bank Securities is that middle and lower income households weren't that far behind. Middle-income households spend 50% on luxuries and even the lowest-income families (the bottom fifth of earners) spend 40%. Like never before, we have bought into the belief that things provide happiness, yet our history is littered with people who achieved great success, accumulating vast possessions, without ever finding happiness.

What is wrong with our world when H.G. Wells, after achieving world fame as a writer and historian, writes: "I have no peace. All life is at the end of a tether"? ... when Howard Hughes, after becoming one of the world's wealthiest tycoons, holes himself up in eccentric seclusion for years and finally dies of malnutrition? ... when a well-known U.S. Senator, after his meteoric rise to the top, is divorced by his wife who says "our marriage simply died"? ... when Earnest Hemingway, the leading writer of his day, and still one of history"s most successful, is haunted by paranoia until he blasts his head apart with a shotgun? ... when a member of one of America's most wealthy families, the Rockefellers, is asked "how much money is enough" and answers "a few dollars more"? ... when Ralph Barton, who some credit as the founder of the political cartoon, leaves this note as he takes his own life: "I have had few difficulties, many friends, great successes; I have gone from wife to wife and from house to house, visited great countries of the world, but I am fed up with inventing devices to fill up twenty-four hours of the day". Unfortunately such successful failures are far from the exception, yet we still buy into the lie that achievement and accumulation equal fulfillment.

Here in chapter four James makes it clear that the problem is not our environment or the system, but our own worldly desires. The haunting question is "What in the world do you want?"

The Cause of Worldliness (4:1-5)

📖 How does worldliness reveal itself according to verse 1?

"What is the source of quarrels and conflicts among you", James asks. The source of our problem with worldliness, according to this passage, is our pleasures or lusts that "wage war within us". James is expanding on a theme he introduced in chapter one — that temptation and sin are driven by our own fallen desires.

📖 What do you think it means for your pleasures to "wage war in your members"?

Have you experienced this?

Pleasures "wage war" (from "*stratos*", an encamped enemy) within us. Our pleasures are waging a war with God's Spirit for control of our hearts. This is the "double-mindedness" spoken of in 1:8 and repeated in 4:8. Although both 1:8 and 4:8 relate our penchant for double-mindedness, the reality of verse 4 is that being double-minded (half for God and fall for the world) is really opposition to God.

📖 What is to blame for worldliness (4:1)?

The Greek word for "pleasures" here is *hedone* from which our English word "hedonism" is derived. A "hedonist" is one who believes that pleasure is the principal good. His or her own desires become the yardstick from which judgments of morality and value are made. The same Greek word is used in the parable of the soils (Luke 8:14) as describing the analogous thorns which choke the seed of the word and make it unfruitful. The obvious point is this: the problem of worldly desires is internal, not external. You don't have to posses great material wealth to be materialistic.

📖 What are the consequences of a pleasure-dominated life (4:2, 3)?

According to this passage, the desires we have aren't necessarily sin. The basic problems arise from a) trying to satisfy those desires ourselves (by committing murder, fighting and quarreling) instead of trusting God (and asking) or b) asking God out of selfish, sinful motives. "Lust" in verse 2 points to passionate desire, a power which if not surrendered to God inevitably sets one person against another. It drives people to shameful deeds: envy, enmity (fighting and quarreling), murder. Verse 3 indicates that a pleasure-dominated life shuts the door on a good prayer life. The true aim of prayer should be "Thy will be done", but the aim of a pleasure-dominated life is "my will be done, my desire be satisfied". In such a state, we are no longer content with what an all-powerful, all-knowing, benevolent God chooses to provide for us.

📖 Compare verse 4 with 2:23. What is the significance of whose friend you are?

James points out in chapter two that friendship with God results in good works. Friendship with the world, he relates here, is hostility toward God. Probably this is an intentional contrast.

📖 Reflect on James' use of the term "adultresses" here and record your thoughts.

Although the KJV translates verse 4 as "ye adulterers and adulteresses", the most trustworthy manuscripts only contain the feminine form ("adulteresses"). The point is that as a believer we are betrothed to Christ. We are His bride, and He is the groom. Worldliness is infidelity to this betrothal. When we become materialistic and pleasure focused we are having an affair with a lover other than Christ. A pleasure-dominated life leads one to a point of dividedness (see 4:8). Remember, this is written to believers. James tells them that friendship with the world (which is under the influence of the evil one, the "god of this world") is hostility toward God.

What is God's desire for us? God desires that He would have all of us and that we would serve Him with a whole heart (James 4:8; Psalm 86:11; Matthew 5:6; Psalm 24:3,4; etc.).

📖 What do you think the quote in verse 5 means practically?

There is some difference of opinion as to exactly what this verse is saying. If you take the word "spirit" to refer to a human's spirit then the message is that "the fallen spirit in us lusts toward envy". A second option, which I hold to, is that the word "spirit" refers to the Holy Spirit (a conclusion the NASB translators drew as reflected by it being capitalized). If this is so, then the message is that the Spirit (the Holy Spirit) who dwells in us, jealously longs to be in control of us (instead of our lusts).

The Cure for Worldliness (4:6-10)

📖 Why is God opposed to the proud, and why does He give grace to the humble?

To be proud (*huperphanos* in the Greek, from *huper*, above, and *phainomai*, to appear or be manifest) signifies showing oneself above others, seeking to be pre-eminent. Pride is rooted in confidence in self, self-sufficiency and self-control, while God desires us to live in dependence on Him. He is "opposed to the proud" – the implication of this statement is that pride is at the root of worldliness. It is ironic, but the way to receive is not to pursue, but to yield. God does not help those who help themselves (as Ben Franklin said); God helps those who come to the end of themselves. When we humble ourselves, then He gives, not as our flesh desires, but in His infinite wisdom He gives exactly what we need. As Romans 12:2 puts it, the will of God is always "good, acceptable and perfect".

Both God's opposition to the proud and His giving to the humble are in the present tense in the Greek. In other words, God stands in continual opposition to the proud, and continually gives grace to the humble. The proud are resisted and the humble are rewarded.

We must remember what James has already taught in chapter 1 about temptation. The problem in temptation is not external, but internal. Every crime in this world has come from desire which was at first only a feeling in the heart, but which, being nourished long enough, came in the end to action.

📖 What was the sin that caused Satan to be cast out of heaven (see Isaiah 14:12-14)?

Satan was cast out of heaven because of pride and arrogance. Instead of accepting the position assigned to him, he said in his heart, "I will make myself like the Most High" (i.e. I want the seat of God). The cure for worldliness is to repent of the pride which insists on having its way, and humble ourselves before God. When we do, we enjoy an unending flow of grace.

📖 What action is required on our part to combat worldliness according to 4:7?

How do I cure my worldly heart? James gives us the solution. The first call of this verse is that we would submit (lit. subject) ourselves to God. The word "submit" here (*hupotasso*) is a military term meaning "to place yourself in order under", as a soldier would his captain. This word appears in the "imperative" mood meaning that it is a command, not a suggestion. When we place ourselves under God's rule and reign, we are protected and provided for, but like an umbrella, if we step out from under it, we lose its protection. Submission to God is the heart attitude which says, "Not my will, but Thine be done". It is an act of trust that God's will really is "good, acceptable and perfect" as His word says it is in Romans 12:2.

A key to walking with God is not just submission to His will, but also to His way. When Satan tempted Jesus in the wilderness, he was offering things which were God's will (that Jesus be fed, that Jesus be protected, that Jesus have rule over the world - see Matthew 4:1-11). The problem was that Satan was wanting to provide God's will in his own way, with his own shortcuts. Submission to God means waiting for Him to provide, not taking matters into our own hands and being self-sufficient.

The second action word here is to "resist." This word (*antistete*) is also a military term. It means "to stand in array as in a battle; to take your stand against". When I submit to God, I have just resisted the devil. His primary goal is to incite me to rebellion just as he has rebelled. When I choose to submit to God I am turning my back on Satan's temptation. Conversely, it is impossible to resist the devil without submitting to God. They are not two separate acts per se. You cannot do one without the other. The great promise of this verse is that when I do turn my back on Satan by submitting to God, he always turns his tail and runs.

📖 Is it possible to "submit to God" without "resisting the devil" or vice versa?

No, the two go hand in hand. It is impossible to resist the devil apart from the empowering of God that we receive when we submit to Him. You can't follow both God and Satan – to say no to God is to say yes to Satan and vice versa.

📖 What approach is required in submitting to God (4:8)?

We must draw near to God, and the only way to do this is by cleansing our hands and purifying our hearts. As Hebrews 10:22 puts it, "Let us draw near...having our hearts sprinkled clean from an evil conscience and our bodies washed with pure water." The Greek word for "draw near" here is (*eggizo*) means "to come close." It has the idea of communion with God; walking in fellowship with Him.

📖 What is the difference between "cleansing your hands" and "purifying your heart" in your opinion?

"Cleansing your hands" has to do with actions while "Purifying your heart" has to do with attitudes. The focus of this exhortation to "cleanse your hands" is on dealing with outward defilement. In other words, deal with the specific acts of sin that creep up in your life throughout the day. Confess them to the Lord and repent of them. With "purify your hearts" the focus shifts to the inner attitudes which are just as displeasing to the Lord, and which, left unchecked, will eventually show up in the actions. There is also a need to unite our hearts under one banner. "Double-minded" literally means "two-souled" and carries the idea of "divided allegiance" – half for God and half for the world."

📖 What attitude does this submission James calls for require (4:9)?

James tells us to "be miserable and mourn and weep." This exhortation is reminiscent of the Sermon on the Mount where Jesus says "Blessed are those who mourn, for they shall be comforted" (Matthew 5:4). The mourning spoken of is that which results from poverty of spirit or humility (see Matthew 5:3) and is the attitude we are to have toward our sin. When we are miserable and mourn and weep over our sin (true heart repentance) we are exalted by the Lord (lifted up) and we are given grace according to 4:6. James isn't advocating "spiritual masochism", but rather, he is calling for a serious attitude about our sins.

📖 Compare verse 10 with verse 6. Why the repetition?

The attitudes and actions of verses 7-9 are adequately summarized in the concept of humility before God. We need to humble ourselves before God (which is the only logical attitude to have in light of His sovereign, omnipotent position) and leave our own exaltation to His discretion and timing. James has already taught that God desires humility, and now in verse 10 he is exhorting us to act on what we know.

Personal Application

Most of us would shudder at the thought of committing adultery and yet in verse 4 James makes it clear that friendship with the world is spiritual adultery. It is "hostility toward God." James warns against being "double-minded" (literally "two-souled"), which basically means having divided allegiance. God wants our whole heart, not half-hearted devotion. Consider the following questions as you appraise your own spiritual condition.

1. "What in the world do you want?" Circle those things you desire that hinder your walk with God. (They may be things you already have)

a) Money   b) Possessions   c) Honors
d) Position   e) Mate   f) Fame
g) Power   h) Sex   i) Other

2. Have you prayed about these desires (see Philippians 4:6,7)? If not, why not?

3. In II Timothy 4 there is an interesting contrast. In verse 8 Paul refers to all those "who have loved His appearing." In verse 10 he refers to Demas as "having loved this present world." Use the grid below to indicate where your heart is right now.

Love His appearing   1 2 3 4 5 6 7 Love this present world

4. What things need to be dealt with as you seek to "purify your heart"?

a) Attitudes

b) Actions

LESSON TEN

"THE PROBLEM OF PLAYING GOD"

James 4:10-5:6

In 1923, a very important meeting was held at the Edgewater Beach Hotel in Chicago. Attending this meeting were nine who would become the world's most successful financiers: Charles Schwab, became president of the largest independent steel company; Samuel Insull, president of the largest utility company; Howard Hopson, president of the largest gas company; Arthur Cotton, the greatest wheat speculator; Richard Whitney, president of the New York stock exchange; Albert Fall, a member of the President's Cabinet; Leon Fraser, president of the bank of International Settlements; Jesse Livermore, the greatest "bear" on Wall Street; and Ivar Krueger, head of the greatest monopoly.

Twenty-five years later, Charles Schwab had died in bankruptcy, having lived on borrowed money for five years before his death; Samuel Insull had died a fugitive from justice, and penniless in a foreign land; Howard Hopson was insane; Arthur Cotton had died abroad, insolvent; Richard Whitney had spent time in Sing Sing; Albert Fall had been pardoned so that he could die at home; Leon Fraser, Jesse Livermore, and Ivar Krueger had all died by suicide. All of these men had learned well the art of making a living, but none of them had learned HOW TO LIVE!

God has made us for Himself. As St. Augustine said centuries ago, "Thou hast made us for Thyself, O God, and our hearts are restless until they find their rest in Thee."

The Characteristics of Autonomy from God (4:10-17)

📖 What does it mean to "speak against" a brother? (use a Greek dictionary if possible)

One of the first places a worldly heart shows up is on our tongues. If our heart is toward the world we will not get along with those who are walking with God. Speak against (*katalaleo*) means to speak evil of, to slander with whatever words come to one's mouth without giving thought to them. The command not to do this is in the "Present Imperative" tense which when used in the negative prohibiting an action usually carries with it the implication of stopping an action that has been taking place.

📖 Why is it wrong to judge a brother?

One way a heart toward the world reveals itself is in judgmental attitudes. If we are walking in the way of the world, instead of humility there will be pride, and we will begin to draw our worth from comparing ourselves to those around us. Because such an attitude is rooted in the world and not in God, we will always judge in such a way that the sin of the other is magnified and ours is belittled. This is what the Pharisee was doing in Luke 18:9-14 (the parable of the Pharisee and the Publican). A worldly heart focuses on other's faults, but a heart after God's heart sees only our own sin and God's grace.

📖 Is it ever right to judge a brother? (explain your answer)

Only God who is sovereign can judge rightly and with justice, yet sometimes He chooses to exercise that right through a human agency (e.g. the Jewish Legal system, Deuteronomy 16:18-22; Romans 13:1-7; Titus 3:1; etc.). Even then though, it must be exercised in the fear of God (Hebrews 13:17) and only when using God-given authority – not in our general relationships (your neighbor or brethren).

📖 What "law" is James speaking of in verse 11? (justify your answer)

James may have in view here the Mosaic Law, the Jewish Legal system, but more likely has in mind the "Royal Law" (Matthew 22:36-40; 7:12) which when accomplished, fulfills the other and deals specifically with our relationships.

📖 What is the significance of verse 12 in this context?

"There is only one Lawgiver and Judge", verse 12 relates. James' point here is that only the one who gave the Law has a right to hold people accountable to it. The good news here is that the Lawgiver is not only able to punish, but also to save or rescue from punishment. When we judge, we can destroy but we can never save. Romans 14:4 states, "Who are you to judge the servant of another? To his own master he stands or falls; and stand he will, for the Lord is able to make him stand." Verse 12 could well be paraphrased "Who do you think you are to judge your neighbor?" Since God gave the law and will one day call all men into account to it, we should leave all judgements to Him. He is able to save and destroy with true justice (requiring omniscience, omnipotence, and omnipresence). For us to judge others is to elevate ourselves to the position of God – something Satan was cast out of heaven for doing.

📖 Compare this passage with 1 Corinthians 4:1-5.

One of the reasons God does not allow us to judge is because we are unable to do it fairly. "Rare is the man who can weigh the faults of another without putting his finger on the scales." In 1 Corinthians 4:5 Paul shows us how God judges: He will "bring to light the things hidden in darkness and disclose the motives of men's hearts." We are unfit to judge because we can never do it fairly. There is always something hidden we do not see, and there is no way for us to see the heart motive. To judge our brother or sister is to "play God" in their lives. It implies we are placing ourselves in the superior position of Judge and Lawgiver which belongs only to God. Paul doesn't even examine himself (not speaking of healthy self-evaluation, but rather, "to closely scrutinize with a view to judgement"). He leaves that to God. Since God is resident in every believer's life then He is able to examine us in the present (Holy Spirit's conviction) as well as at time's end.

📖 What is wrong with the statement in verse 13?

The scenario begins, "Come now, you who say...". The problem here is not making plans. There is nothing sinful about making plans. The problem here is excluding God from those plans. Failing to acknowledge His sovereignty over all is another manifestation of worldliness. The itinerant merchants spoken of here with the term "you" were Jews who carried on a lucrative trade throughout the world. Planning without praying is arrogant boasting according to verse 16.

📖 Verse 16 identifies this statement as "arrogant boasting." Why is this so?

The statement of verse 16 is arrogant boasting because it assumes tomorrow as a right instead of a gift of God's grace. It is the pride of independence and autonomy (self-rule). James' point here is that it is presumptuous to boast of tomorrow, for God has not promised tomorrow to any of us. Whenever we make plans, we must yield to the fact that God can and sometimes will overrule them. To not allow God this role is to deny His Lordship. Proverbs 27:1 says, "Do not boast about tomorrow, for you do not know what a day may bring forth." The boasting spoken of here is not necessarily verbal. It is the boasting of a life that is autonomous from God and self-sufficient. James says, "all such boasting is evil."

📖 What are the explanations James gives in verse 14?

We don't know what tomorrow holds since we are not sovereign like God. We have no promise of tomorrow – we are just a passing vapor (this has the idea of your breath on a cold morning that appears for just a moment).

📖 Why is verse 15 a better statement than verse 13?

Verse 15 is a better statement than verse 13 because it allows for the sovereign intervention of God. It gives room for His rule in our lives (see 2 Corinthians 1:15-20). Instead, we ought to say, "If the Lord wills…" we shall do this or that. We can see that this is a superior statement because it reflects a recognition of God's sovereign control. We see this attitude illustrated by Paul in 2 Corinthians 1:15-20; Acts 18:21; 1 Corinthians 4:19, 16:7.

📖 What exactly is James saying in verse 17?

Here James makes much the same point as in 1:22 and makes it a little more forcefully. "To one who knows the right thing to do and does not do it, to him it is sin." Here James shows that sin is not merely a breaking of God's commandments. It is also a neglect of God's expectations. Not simply an act of commission, sin may be an act of omission as it is here. The exhortation rings back to what James said in 1:19-27. Unapplied knowledge is sin, so we should be cautious of seeking knowledge as an end in itself. To know and not to do is sin - knowledge brings a greater accountability.

📖 How does verse 17 fit in this context?

The specific things we are accountable to do from this passage are: a) to not "play God" in others lives (by judging and speaking against them) and b) to not "play God" with our own life (by operating autonomously and neglecting to involve God in all our plans).

📖 What does this verse imply about knowledge as an end in itself?

Unapplied knowledge is sin so we should guard against seeking knowledge as an end in itself. Otherwise we call ourselves into a greater accountability before God.

The Consequence of Autonomy from God (5:1-6)

📖 What does this passage say will happen to worldly treasures?

Worldly treasures will not last. They will rot, become moth-eaten, and rust, and their temporality will be a witness against the rich person and will consume them. (may have in mind eternal damnation but more likely refers to his possessions possessing him and binding his affections to this world).

📖 What is the real problem of these verses?

One of the reasons worldliness is wrong is because it's value is temporary, not eternal. James warns, "Your riches have rotted and your garments have become moth-eaten." Both of these verbs are in the perfect tense meaning action that is already complete. James' point is, "you are treasuring that which is corrupted and defiled, and you are clothing yourselves with that which is moth-eaten and worthless in light of eternity." Whatever is not eternal is eternally insignificant. The real issue is not how much wealth we possess, but how much our wealth possesses us. Under what circumstances would the situation in verses 1-3 not devastate a rich person? Only if the object of his trust was God instead of his riches. Since wealth is not eternal it only has lasting value as it is used to accomplish eternal things.

📖 What is the significance of storing up treasures in the "last days" (verse 3)?

The verse literally reads "ye treasured in the last days" which is illogical since the treasures spoken of are not eternal (See Luke 12:15-20). In other words, "Why store up treasures if it is the last days?"

📖 What is the point of verse 4?

The rich man James speaks of is not just anyone with wealth but the one who has obtained that wealth at the expense of others. That means ill-gotten gain is a witness to God against such a one.

📖 What does the title "Lord of Sabaoth" mean?

What insight does that give you into the meaning of that verse?

"The Lord of Sabaoth" is a transliterated Hebrew term meaning "the Lord of Hosts" or "the Lord all sovereign." The Lord Almighty, the omnipotent sovereign, is not oblivious to injustice. One of the reasons James is so hard on the rich is because it is very difficult to become rich without it being at someone else's expense. Either we gain wealth by charging too much and defrauding, or we hoard wealth by not giving as we should to the needs of others. Wealth gotten by injustice cannot be hidden from the "all-sovereign Lord". The rich man who says "God doesn't see" is just as foolish as the child who covers his eyes and says "you can't see me".

📖 What does the statement "you have fattened your hearts in a day of slaughter" mean?

James' statement about fattening hearts in a day of slaughter is probably an allusion to Jeremiah 12:1-3. The luxurious rich who get wealth by injustice and spend it on their pleasures are fattening themselves like sheep unconscious of their doom. This idea stands in sharp contrast to the call of verse 8 to "strengthen your hearts, for the coming of the Lord is at hand".

📖 What is the meaning of verse 6?

The rich man has taken advantage of and looked down upon the righteous man and is not resisted – probably because of the exhortation in verse 7, which seems to be directed to the righteous man. He doesn't resist the rich man because God will judge at his return.

📖 Compare verse 6 with 2:6, 7.

Perhaps this practice of the rich oppressing the poor and taking them to court is what James has in mind when he speaks of condemning and putting to death the righteous man. Selfishness and greed motivates the rich to take the poor ("the righteous") to court to take away what little they might have by legal trickery, instead of simply absorbing the loss with their abundance. This action amounted to "murdering" the poor.

Personal Application

One of the most dangerous trends of modern Christianity is the shift toward Christian autonomy. Believers want all the blessings of Christ but they don't want any personal responsibility. They have bought into the mentality of Western "Meism" where people don't want to be accountable to anyone—not to parents, not to Government, not to society, and especially not to God. It is a step beyond simple materialism and worldliness. In this philosophy, rather than man serving God, he attempts to manipulate God to meet his own desires. The result is alienation from others and ultimately God. The real challenge of James in this passage is "Let God be God in your life" - submit to His sovereignty and will. That is the essence of "humbling yourself?" (verse 10).

1. Do you rebel at the thought of being accountable to God for everything you do? (if so, why?)

2. Do you tend to speak against others out of need to build yourself up?

3. Do you secretly enjoy the misfortunes and/or the sins of others and seek to magnify them?

4. Do you tend to leave God out of your plans so you can boast of your own accomplishments?

5. How do you feel when you consider the fact that tomorrow is uncertain and your life is a vapor?

6. What is your attitude toward the will of God?

7. What do you need to do in order to stop playing God?

LESSON ELEVEN

"STANDING TALL OVER THE LONG HAUL"

James 5:7-12

An interesting experiment was performed by the late Johns Hopkins professor Curt Richter researching the impact that hope has on performance. In the 1950s, he conducted a gruesome experiment with rats. He first took a control group of domesticated rats, put them into jars half filled with water, and observed them. The idea was to measure how long they swam before they gave up and drowned. One by one, he placed rats into the water. Surprisingly, within minutes of entering the water, all of them died. It appeared that once they had concluded that their situation was hopeless, a result of the failed attempt to discover any viable escape, the rats all gave up. Then the scientists introduced a variable into the experiment. They would let the rats frantically search for a means of escape until they reached that point of giving up, and then the scientists would "rescue" the rat by pulling it out of the water for a short time and then they would place it back into the water. What they discovered was that by interjecting the hope of rescue, the rat's entire performance was altered. It would swim in circles for hours until it was physically incapable of continuing. The only difference in the performance of the two groups was the added element of hope.

This seems to be James' key that he isolates here in chapter five as he addresses the subject of endurance. The key to endurance, he teaches, is realizing that the coming of the Lord is at hand. That is what keeps us going in the Christian life, for that is our hope.

The Essence of Endurance (5:7-8)

📖 Is the phrase "be patient" an option or a command, and what is the significance of this?

While it may not seem totally definitive in English, the phrase "be patient" is a command (aorist imperative) in the original Greek and not an option. Literally, the term is "long tempered" (Greek – *makrothumeo* from *makro*, "long", *thumeo*, "temper" or "anger"). Fortunately, Galatians 5:22-23 identifies patience as part of the "fruit of the Spirit" – an evidence of God's rule and reign in our lives. Conversely, apart from God's rule in our lives, patience is an impossibility. In 4:1-3 we see that worldliness is characterized by impatience.

📖 How do some of the other topics of this book relate to this one?

Most prominent among the topics James addresses would be the need for endurance in trials (chapter 1). Conversely, the negative issues addressed in chapters 2-4 evidence a lack of patience and eternal perspective.

📖 James illustrates his definition of patience by relating it to the farmer. What insights can you draw from this comparison?

James illustrates his definition of patience by relating it to the farmer. Some insights that can be drawn from this comparison are: a) patience is a necessity since he is dependent on the workings of another and upon time. Christ's return, and the hope that accompanies it, is likewise out of our control, b) the patience's of a farmer must be lived out day by day ("being patient about it" is in the Greek present tense meaning continuous repeated action) just as our patience for the Lord's return. The early rains occur in October – November and the late rains in April – May as Palestine has two rainy seasons.

📖 Why does James tell us to "strengthen our hearts"?

James calls to "strengthen your hearts" because "the coming of the Lord is at hand" and a strong heart is necessary to endure until then. This exhortation to "strengthen your hearts" stands as a stark contrast to the materialists who "fatten" their hearts.

📖 Identify all references to patience or endurance in verses 7-12.

Notice the references to patience and endurance here: "be patient" (5:7), "being patient" (5:7), "be patient" (5:8), "patience" (5:10), "endured" (5:11), "endurance" (5:11). Vine's Dictionary identifies the meaning of the exhortation "be patient" as this: "Patience is the quality that does not surrender to circumstances or succumb to trial; it is the opposite of despondency and is associated with hope" (Vine's Expository Dictionary, p. 694).

The Extent of Endurance (5:7-8)

📖 How long is the believer commanded to be patient and why? The believer is exhorted to be patient "until the coming of the Lord" because true patience is associated with hope. It is essential that we keep in view "the coming of the Lord" since that is our hope. The phrase "coming of the Lord" literally reads "presence of the Lord". The term is generally used to designate the arrival of a ruler.

📖 What effect does this mentality have on the way you live your life?

Verse 7 begins with the term "therefore." This indicates that what James is saying is tightly linked with what precedes it. The word is usually associated with applications that flow out of a truth, and/or conclusions that should be drawn. As we keep in view "the coming of the Lord," we develop an eternal mindset and begin to evaluate life more accurately. The "big picture" of eternity gives the proper context for establishing our priorities.

📖 Is enduring possible without expecting?

It is not really possible to endure without expecting. It has been said that man can live 3 months without food, 3 days without water, and 3 minutes without air but not a second without hope. It is our expectation of the Lord's return that gives us the strength to endure.

📖 Compare this passage with Hebrews 11:9-10, 24-27, and 12:1-4, keeping in mind the theme of endurance.

Abraham endured by looking for what God had promised (verse 10). Likewise, Moses was able to endure because he was "looking to the reward" and because he saw "Him who is unseen". In Hebrews 12:1-4 we see that the way we "run with endurance" is by focusing on our hope – Jesus Christ. This prevents us from growing weary and losing heart. Likewise, Christ gave us an example by enduring the cross "for the joy set before Him".

The Evidence of Endurance (5:9,12)

📖 How does not complaining against one another fit in with endurance?

To complain means to "grumble, sigh, or moan because of an undesirable circumstance" and therefore would be the opposite of enduring in a situation. As we learned in chapter 1, in every trial we either endure ("to remain under", "to go the distance") or we try to escape.

📖 Does complaining reveal a lack of patience, and if so, how?

Grumbling and complaining reflects a loss of patience because it fails to recognize the sovereign rule of God. If God is both sovereign and graciously committed to us then we can accept every circumstance as being directly from Him and filtered through His will. (See Romans 8:28; Job 1; etc.)

📖 What does swearing have to do with patience or the second coming?

To "swear" as James addresses here refers not to "curse" words or crude slang, but to the practice of making false vows. The idea of making vows is not in itself a negative, but only when done in a flippant, profane or blasphemous way. Solemn vows or covenants can be made, but in light of the Lord's return and our giving an account to Him, must be followed through on. Our yes should mean yes and should not be self-serving rhetoric.

📖 Compare verse 12 with Matthew 23:16.

In these passages, as well as the companion passage James is probably drawing on here (Matthew 5:33-37), Jesus addresses the pharisaical practice of leaving loopholes with their vows (kind of like having your fingers crossed). The point is there is no escaping God, so our word is required to stand with integrity at all times. Life is lived before God, not just before men.

📖 What significance would false vows hold in light of the imminent return of our Lord?

False vows are pretty foolish in light of the imminent return of the Lord, a day in which all will give account to God. A good parallel to the oath taking of Jesus' day would be contracts today. We should not use the absence of a legally binding contract as an excuse for not keeping our word, because we are still accountable to God for integrity. Christ may have had false vows in mind in His rebuke to the Pharisees in Matthew 12:36-37.

The Example of Endurance (5:10-11)

📖 How are the prophets an example of suffering and patience?

How are they able to do it?

The prophets serve as a good example of suffering and patience because they suffered persecution for being faithful to God and were patient, recognizing Him as the highest authority and the one to whom they would have to answer. James may have in view Jesus' words in the Sermon on the Mount (see Matthew 5:11-12). The prophets of old were able to endure suffering with patience by focusing on God and having Him as their audience. They were "looking for the blessed hope" (Titus 2:13), and the reward for their deeds.

📖 What did Job endure?

What was the "outcome of the Lord's dealings ?"

Job endured the loss of all his possessions which were many (Job 1:12-17), the loss of his children (Job 1:18-19), the loss of his health (Job 2:7-8), and the unenlightened judgements of his wife (Job 2:9-

10) and friends (Job 2:11-31:40). The outcome of the Lord's dealings with Job do show His mercy and great compassion. He restored Job's possessions twofold (Job 42:10), He restored Job's health fully and extended his life (Job 42:16-17), and He restored Job's children twofold (Job 42:13-15) since he not only had ten new children but would be reunited with the ten who died in heaven.

📖 How do these Old Testament examples James mentions present a good Biblical model for us today?

In each and every case endurance was accomplished by focusing on hope and keeping their eyes on God. James' examples demonstrate clearly the necessity of living life with an eternal perspective.

📖 What does this passage reveal about the character of God?

James explains to us that our Lord is "full of compassion" (literally "very compassionate" – the Greek word, *splanchnon*, means to be moved inwardly) and is "merciful" (literally "pitiful", the Greek word, *oiktirmon*, from "*oiktos*", meaning pity). "*Oi*", an exclamation, is the equivalent of our expression, "Oh!", and has the idea of compassion toward the ills of others with a view toward action.

Personal Application

One of the greatest evidences of the reality of our faith is patience—patience with trials, with others, with ourselves, with God. In Galatians 5:22-23 Paul identifies patience as "fruit of the Spirit." In this passage James shows us our need for patience, not as an end in itself, but for "meantime" living. Christ is definitely coming, but in the meantime what we really need is patient endurance. Patience is not so much the subject as it is the application to the subject of the coming of the Lord. Fortunately it is not something we have to manufacture but something God produces in us as we respond rightly to the trials He places in our lives. With this in mind it isn't so hard to "consider them all joy."

1. How would you rate your own personal patience level?

Enduring   1   2   3   4   5   6   7   8   9   Complaining

2. Does the fact that Christ could come again at any moment affect your patience level?

3. Is your grumbling or complaining against others the result of frustration with someone or something else?

4. Do you try to cover up your true heart by reacting to difficulties defensively, by using spiritual jargon, or even making bargains with God?

5. What situations are you facing in life right now that require patience?

6. How can you apply this passage to those situations?

LESSON TWELVE

"THE PRACTICE OF PRAYING"

James 5:13-20

The great hymn writer, Fanny Crosby, though blinded in infancy, greeted friends and strangers alike with a cheerful "God bless your dear soul!" And, according to her own statement, she never attempted to write a hymn without first kneeling in prayer. Assuming this is true, Fanny Crosby spent considerable time on her knees. She wrote no less than 8,000 songs. Miss Crosby was often under pressure to meet deadlines. It was under such circumstances in 1869 that she tried to write words for a tune Composer W.H. Doane had sent her. But she couldn't write. Then she remembered she had forgotten her prayer. Rising from her knees, she dictated – as fast as her assistant could write - words for the famous hymn, "Jesus, Keep Me Near the Cross".

But one day in 1874, Fanny Crosby prayed for more material things. She had run short of money and needed five dollars – even change. There was no time to draw on her publishers, so she simply prayed for the money. Her prayer ended, she was walking to and fro in her room trying to get "in the mood" for another hymn when an admirer called. Greeting the stranger with "God bless your dear soul", the two chatted briefly. In the parting handshake the admirer left something in the hymn-writer's hand. It was five dollars. Rising from a prayer of thanks the blind poetess wrote: "All the way my Savior leads me."

The Reasons for Prayer (5:13-14)

📖 James exhorts anyone who is suffering to pray. In light of chapter 1, why is this so important?

Trials and suffering create a need in our lives for wisdom. God's wisdom is made available to us through prayer (1:5) and is necessary if we are to persevere and endure. The Greek word used here for "suffering" (*kakopathei*) means "to undergo hardship, to be afflicted, to suffer trouble". James uses this general term because all suffering, be it mental, physical, emotional, or spiritual, should drive us to our knees in honest conversation with God. Peter gives us the reason: "casting all your anxiety upon Him, because He cares for you" (1 Peter 5:7). When we suffer, we are to "pray." This word (*proseuchomai*) embraces all that is included in the idea of prayer: thanks, asking, requesting special things. The prefix, *pros*, implies praying to God. Prayer is not really prayer unless it is connected communication with God. Unless my heart is right, my sins are dealt with, and my trust is in Him, I am simply talking to myself.

📖 What would the opposite of praying be in a situation of suffering?

Trying to manipulate our own solution through self-effort or by trusting any solution other than God. It mirrors the contrast in chapter one of listening to God verses listening to ourselves.

📖 If one is cheerful, why does he need to be exhorted to sing praises?

Need is not the only reason to pray. If I only talk with God when I need something, that isn't much of a relationship. This exhortation underscores our basic tendency, also addressed in 4:13-17, to forget God and to take all credit for success when all is going well. By singing praises we recognize the sovereign role of God in all the blessings we experience. Thankfulness is a sign of gratitude. James' key point is this: that if anyone finds themselves in any of these circumstances, he or she should, by prayer, include and intimately involve God in their situation. Since we are always in adversity or blessing, we ought always to pray.

📖 Of what benefit is involving others in the prayer process when you're sick?

When we are sick, James commands us to involve others in praying (5:16). Doing so allows us to draw on them as a source of encouragement, wisdom and counsel. Asking others to pray strengthens the interdependence of the body. It also builds the faith of others as God works.

Although the context implies physical sickness, the word is much more general, and so too, the principle. It is right and appropriate to be drawn to my knees by the need of another. In the original Greek text verse 14 begins with a statement rather than a question, and should be rendered, "Someone among you is sick". James begins the discussion with the fact that there is sickness in the world and the Christian is not exempt.

Scripture lists at least five different reasons for sickness. One reason is to bring glory to God through miraculous healing (John 9:1-3). A second reason could be as a trial to cause a believer's growth and dependence on God (Job 2:7-8; 2 Corinthians 12:8). Sickness could also be used to call God's child to repentance from sin (individual sin – Psalm 38:3; parent's sin – John 9:2-3 [inferred]; a leader's sin – Exodus 9:8-17; and the sins of a nation – 2 Chronicles 7:14). Related to this, sickness could be used to judge sin (our own sin – 1 Corinthians 11:30; our parent's sin – 2 Samuel 12:15; a leader's sin – 1 Chronicles 21:8-17; and the sins of a nation – Isaiah 1:4-8). A final reason for sickness could be as God's means of calling me home to heaven (John 11:4 by inference).

📖 What is the significance of each of these situations in the midst of a life of faith and obedience?

James' point seems to be that if anyone finds himself in any of those circumstances he should, by prayer, intimately involve God in them.

The Requirements for Prayer (5:14-16)

📖 Why should the Church and its leadership be involved in our difficulties?

To the one who is sick James exhorts, "Let him call for the elders of the church." Notice that the one who is sick initiates this, not the elders. Why involve the elders? Perhaps because as we just saw, sickness results from many different causes. It takes men of wisdom and authority to discern the real need. If the purpose of the sickness is to glorify God through it's healing, then the church should be a witness to that. If the sickness results from sin, we will need men of wisdom who are able to "exhort in sound doctrine" (Titus 1:9) to put us on the right track. That certainly seems to be the inference of the last part of verse 15.

📖 What is the significance of anointing the sick person "with oil in the name of the Lord"?

Anointing with oil, although a spiritual practice, was primarily an accepted medicinal practice of the day (as illustrated in Luke 10:34 – the treating of the victim by the good Samaritan). The point seems to be "use all help available to you" (which in our day would include doctors and technology), but do so "in the name of the Lord". In other words, trust God for the results, not just the medicine and treatments. The Greek construction clarifies the order. The word translated "anointing him" term describes an act which precedes the prayer and should be translated "having anointed".

📖 Are prayers of faith answered simply because they are prayed in faith?

Prayers of faith are not answered affirmatively simply because they are prayed in faith. The key point here is that God – not the prayer, nor the medicine, nor the faith, but God – is the one who raises them up. Faith is simply trusting God. It is not the strength of the faith or the amount of faith (be it large or mustard seed sized) but the faithfulness of what it is placed in that makes the difference. Unfortunately, many who have misinterpreted passages like this one find themselves advocating faith in faith or faith in prayer rather than faith in God. Prayers of faith are answered not simply because they are prayed in faith but only if they are prayed in the will of God. (see 1 John 5:14).

📖 Why do you think James adds the statement "and the Lord will raise him up"?

God must do the work, and we must surrender to His sovereignty. We cannot have biblical faith that God "will" heal someone unless that is God's will. Clearly Scripture teaches that healing temporally is not always God's will. In fact, all earthly healing is imperfect because it is temporal. Even Lazarus, who was raised from the dead, died again. The ultimate healing is when God calls me home and glorifies my sin-stained body. A key point however, is this should not be used as an excuse for not trusting God. We must believe that what the word teaches is true, namely, God IS able to heal. Probably James adds this phrase to keep us from thinking that it was our "prayer offered in faith" that raises the sick one up. Prayer has no mystic power in and of itself – it only serves as a vehicle to communicate with God. Prayer is only powerful because God is powerful, so He must be our focus.

📖 How does forgiveness of sins and confession to others fit into the picture?

Medical science has long recognized the role of forgiveness (or the lack of it) in our mental health. The more research is done, the stronger the link is established between mental and emotional health and our physical health. Obviously, as well, some sickness is directly related to sin as we addressed earlier.

The Results of Prayer (5:16-18)

📖 What according to this passage is effective prayer?

James tells us that effective prayer is that which is prayed by a righteous man. Because the Greek verb used here is a participle, it could also be translated "effective praying". In light of the overall context of the epistle the emphasis in this verse should be placed on the man being righteous, rather than the prayer being effective (see Proverbs 15:8). James' point seems to be this - "If a man is righteous, his prayers will be effective." We tend to make the mistake of trying to organize an effective prayer life instead of realizing that this will come as we become more righteous.

The Greek word translated "effective" in vs. 16 is "*energeo*" (from which our English word "energy" is derived) and means to be active, powerful, or strong. Spiros Zodhiates in his "Lexicon to the New Testament" says this of this word, "In James 5:16 it seems to denote the inspired prayer of the prayer of a righteous man wrought by the operation or energy of the Holy Spirit (cf. Romans 8:26,27)" ("Hebrew/Greek Key Study Bible", S. Zodhiates, AMG Publishers, 1984, p. 1689).

📖 Does verse 16 mean that if you follow this Biblical formula you will always be healed? (justify your answer)

While the doctrine of "universal healing" is true Biblically, it is often misapplied. God will heal all our diseases ultimately but in many cases this will not be until heaven. God is not creating an "earthly Utopia," for we would not long for heaven if earth held only joy. He is working from and for eternity. Death serves as the ultimate act of healing as it releases us from eternal bondage to our sinful nature and thus "heals" us. The healing spoken of here is probably sickness resulting from sin.

📖 What is the significance of Elijah being a "man with a nature like ours"?

Although a very righteous man, he was still just a man with a fallen, sinful nature like us. He was not some elitist "super saint" but just a man who walked with God. Therefore we too can experience the victorious prayer life that he had.

📖 Verse 17 says Elijah didn't just pray but he "prayed earnestly." What does it take to define prayer as earnest?

By looking at the Old Testament passage this refers to (I Kings 17 and 18) we can conclude that it doesn't necessarily mean lengthy prayers or all-night vigils since these were short prayers. The verse is literally translated "in prayer, he prayed," an Hebraism indicating prayer "to God" as opposed to prayer in general. Earnest prayer is serious prayer which reaches God. In all seriousness, what would prevent us from accomplishing the same feat today? God has not changed, but few have taken the time or have made the steps of faith necessary to know and trust God as Elijah did. God still does mighty things but His work is hampered by our lack of faith (Matthew 3:58).

The results James relates here are astounding only because our praying today is often vague, general and impotent. God has not changed, but few have taken the time nor have made the steps of faith necessary to know and trust God as Elijah did. God still does mighty things but He desires to involve us in what He is doing and His work is hampered by our lack of faith (Matthew 13:58). James was nicknamed "Camel Knees" because of the calluses worn from many hours of prayer. Yet the emphasis of his only epistle is not prayer, but genuine faith. Perhaps the reason is that effective prayer flows always and only out of a life of genuine faith or trust in God.

Conclusion (5:19-20)

📖 How does verse 19 fit with the context of the book and its audience?

In many ways the whole book of James is an application of the thought of these last two verses. His goal is to get the Jews of the dispersion "back on track" in their Christian walk.

📖 What do you think is meant in verse 20 by the phrases "save his soul from death", and "cover a multitude of sins"?

Apparently it is possible for a believer to reach such a sinful state that God calls him home early rather than have His name maligned (see 1 Corinthians 11:30 and 1 John 5:16). The phrase "will cover a multitude of sins" probably reflects the results of a repentant heart.

Personal Application

James earned the nick-name "camel knees" because of his commitment to prayer. One would expect an epistle written by "camel knees" to begin with a treatise on prayer, be filled with examples and explanations, and close with a challenging exhortation on the subject. In reality the opposite is true. Other than this brief reference at the end of the book, the subject of prayer is conspicuous in its absence. James chooses rather to deal with the more fundamental subject of "genuine faith." His point seems to be this: "if a man is righteous, his prayer life will be effective. Much like the solution to problems with the tongue, the solution to problems in prayer isn't to focus on our payer life, but to focus on a deepening, genuine faith relationship with God. If we do that, a dynamic prayer life will logically follow.

1. Are you satisfied with your prayer life right now?

2. Do you enjoy messages on prayer that make you feel bad because that is how you think you ought to feel?

3. Do you find yourself trying to organize a more effective prayer life through self-effort by scheduling, notebooks, etc.?

4. How are you doing at developing a deepening, genuine faith relationship with God?

5. What do you need to do differently to be more successful at developing this?

6. Write down your three main application points from the book of James.

ABOUT THE AUTHOR

Eddie Rasnake graduated with honors from East Tennessee State University. He and his wife, Michele, served 7 years with Cru at UVa, James Madison, and as campus director at the University of Tennessee. Eddie left Cru to join Wayne Barber at Woodland Park Baptist Church where he still serves as Senior Associate Pastor. He has authored dozens of books and Bible studies and has published materials in Afrikaans, Albanian, German, Greek, Italian, Romanian, Russian and Telugu. Eddie and his wife Michele live in Chattanooga, Tennessee.

What Christian Leaders have to say about Eddie Rasnake's books:

"I encourage you to make these studies a part of your study of God's Word - I am confident you will be blessed!" – **Dr. Bill Bright**, Founder of Cru

"If you long to understand how God dynamically works in the lives of people like you and me, 'Following God' will be food for your soul." – **John MacArthur**, Pastor-Teacher, Grace Community Church

"These three dear men who love God and love His Word have produced an excellent study that will help you see in real life, flesh and blood examples, the cruciality of 'Following God' fully." – **Kay Arthur**, Executive Director, Precept Ministries International

"A wonderful resource for those who are serious in their Bible Study." – **Adrian Rogers**, Pastor, Bellevue Baptist Church, Memphis, Tennessee

"This study consistently takes the student to the Word of God. A refreshing study that stays true to scripture." – **Henry T. Blackaby**, co-author of Experiencing God

"Throughout my ministry of forty-one years, I have never read anything more fresh and enlightening than this book of knowing and living the will of God." – **Reverend Bill Stafford**, Evangelist, Director, International Congress on Revival

"I highly recommend this book not only to the new believer...but also to the older saint who would like a fresh look at how to discover God's will." – **Jan Silvious**, Author and Speaker

"You won't regret the time you spend reading Eddie Rasnake's book. I count it a privilege to know him personally and work with him. His book will help you read the signposts of decisions correctly and properly." – **Dr. Spiros Zodhiates**, Editor of The Hebrew/Greek Key Study Bible, President Emeritus, AMG International.

"If your heart's desire is to become a devoted follower of Christ, then 'Following God' will serve as a compelling roadmap." – **Joseph Stowell**, President Emeritus, Moody Bible Institute

"Fresh, original, imaginative – and Biblical – were the words that came to mind as I read 'What Should I Do, Lord?' Easy reading makes the principles accessible even to the newest Christian." – **Ron Dunn**, Author and Speaker

"Those who seek to do God's will often make decisions with lifelong impact. The tendency is to want to see our names written in the sky along with specific instructions as to what to do. Eddie Rasnake helps young and old alike understand how to know God's will by seeking God's way." – **Frank Brock**, President Emeritus, Covenant College

"*The Acts of the Holy Spirit* points to ways God worked personally, in the first century, using men and women like us to bring the Good News of Jesus to many people. Uncovering some of His acts of power and creativity in the first century can point us to His possibilities in the twenty-first century. Eddie Rasnake insightfully captures and presents this so that it comes home to us. It mattered then. It matters now. Read, explore, feast, follow!" **– Rick Shepherd,** co-creator, Following God Bible Study series

A STUDY IN AUTHENTIC CHRISTIANITY